CHELATION THERAPY

CHELATION THERAPY

THE REVOLUTIONARY ALTERNATIVE TO HEART SURGERY

LEON CHAITOW N.D., D.O.

Thorsons Publishing Group

First published 1990

British Library Cataloguing in Publication Data

Chaitow, Leon
Chelation therapy: the revolutionary alternative to heart
surgery.
1. Man. Cardiovascular system. Therapy
I. Title
616.106

ISBN 0-7225-2203-7

*Published by Thorsons Publishers Limited,
Wellingborough, Northamptonshire NN8 2RQ, England*

Typeset by Harper Phototypesetters Limited,
Northampton, England
Printed in Great Britain by Hartnolls Limited, Bodmin

1 3 5 7 9 10 8 6 4 2

Contents

Acknowledgement

Sincere thanks are expressed for the help given by the late James Kavanagh, Director of The Chelation Centre Ltd, in providing information for the case histories in Chapter 7.

I dedicate this book to the memory of my late father, Max Chaitow, for whom chelation therapy provided years of additional mobility and well-being.

Introduction

It is nothing less than a scandal that a safe method of treatment which could save tens of thousands of lives annually and quite literally billions of pounds in unnecessary expense is being ignored by mainstream medicine.

The main killer diseases of modern times involve circulatory incompetence and while medicine has certainly addressed these problems via surgery of sometimes heroic complexity and via drugs which have a very mixed track record (as in cholesterol lowering drugs efficiently reducing death from heart disease while increasing the likelihood of an early demise from other causes), it has singularly failed to examine to any degree chelation methods which are proven in value (see later chapters and references), extremely safe in modern application (there were a few problems in the early days when too much was done too fast) and relatively inexpensive.

We challenge any physician worthy of that title to look at chelation with an open mind, to visit a chelation centre, to study the case histories we provide — of which many, many more are available – and then to honestly say that this is not a fine, simple, scientific, valid and efficient method for treating many forms of circulatory disease.

Quite simply, the reasons for the medical blinkers relate to prejudice based on lack of knowledge. Hopefully, if we have done our job even moderately well, there will be enough evidence in this book to stimulate a desire to know more. There are other books which explain the concepts at greater length and there are many research papers which are accessible, if more knowledge is wanted.

If it is not, we ask in heaven's name why not?

In the last few years scientists of international repute such as

Professor Emanuel Cheraskin have examined chelation therapy in a private practice setting (see McDonagh, Rudolph and Cheraskin, 1982a) and have found that not only does chelation therapy do what its proponents claim, but that it seems actually to enhance kidney function rather than damage it – the major negative claim thrown at chelation by doctors (see Chapter 6). It is scandalous that the major killers of modern times are allowed to continue to wreak havoc amongst the citizens of industrialized countries without chelation therapy being available except at private cost and without official medical sanction.

There can be few people who do not have a loved one or colleague affected by one or other form of cardiovascular disease. If enough noise is made by the taxpayers who finance political decisions and ultimately pay for medical care, it will be possible to save millions in National Health costs as well as ensuring longer, happier, more productive lives for thousands of people each year.

Chapter 1

Chelation therapy: is it natural?

How fast and how dramatically we age has a great deal to do with impaired circulatory efficiency. If arteries could be kept supple, prevented from hardening and narrowing, the free flow of blood would be assured and both the risk of a rapid degree of ageing as well as many diseases associated with age – such as forms of cardiovascular degeneration, athero- and arteriosclerosis, peripheral circulatory dysfunction, some types of kidney disease, hypertension, cerebrovascular accidents and premature senility as well as, in many instances, cirrhosis and kidney disease – could be prevented or significantly helped if they already existed.

Supporters of chelation therapy claim just these benefits and yet, despite the many published papers supporting these claims (*see* References), many doctors find such claims for the usefulness of chelation therapy to be controversial, and tend to dismiss out of hand the chance that they might just possibly be accurate.

Prevention and treatment of degenerative diseases

Although chelation therapy for prevention and treatment of degenerative circulatory diseases is practised by hundreds of medical doctors in the USA and Europe, it remains controversial, inasmuch as it is misunderstood, its use being grossly underinvestigated by mainstream medicine except in treating a narrow range of conditions such as lead and other heavy metal toxicity or acute hypercalcaemia (increased calcium levels in the blood). Ironically, as will be explained in later chapters, it was the medical use of chelation therapy in removing toxic metals which first led to the discovery of its hugely beneficial 'side-effects', of dramatically enhanced circulatory function.

Those doctors who have examined chelation therapy in action and who have seen its outstanding results in preventing and reversing so many degenerative diseases, usually change rapidly from critics to supporters of this essentially safe system.

Imagine someone (a loved one, friend, a patient if you are a physician, or even yourself) being in great pain, or being virtually disabled, as a result of chronic circulatory dysfunction. It might be that there is so much narrowing of the blood vessels to the heart muscle itself that any exertion would be enough to produce the agony of angina, a fist-like gripping in the chest, accompanied by severe pain, a vice-like pressure, gasping for breath and almost total helplessness. Or it might be that the circulation to the legs is so impeded that taking just a few steps across the room brings on cramp-like gripping of the muscles of the lower leg, or severe aching of the upper leg, or both. These symptoms can be so severe that only a few steps can be taken before stopping is imperative while the circulation trickles through and the cramp eases (often taking several minutes), followed by a few more staggering steps as the cycle of intermittent claudication repeats itself. Or it might be that the abilities to function at all, perhaps to speak or to use one or other limb, or even to be able to think rationally, have been largely lost due to impeded circulation to the brain.

Imagine any one of these catastrophes and consider what options remain open to the person facing this hell.

What choices are there?

Chelation is one. In several hundreds of thousands of cases such as those briefly listed above, chelation therapy has helped to restore normal function.

It does not always do so, damage may be too severe and irreversible. But it offers a chance for a very safe form of intervention which can often take the person involved to the stage where surgery and increased medication become unnecessary and where effective long-term preventive methods, including exercise and dietary strategies, can be introduced.

Is chelation natural?

Given the nature of the damage which has already taken place in such conditions, of the dangers which apply and of the emergency status existing in many such cases, it is as natural an option as is likely to be found, and is certainly the safest.

What does medicine have to offer?

Many of the problems listed above relate specifically to obstruction, to the impeding of the flow of blood, often caused directly by the presence of concretions in the lining of major arteries.

Drugs can certainly help, but frequently at the cost of severe side-effects, and none address the causes of the problem, thus leaving the likelihood of the development of further disasters. Certainly there are now a host of drugs of varying degrees of effectiveness, all of which have major side-effects and some of which, while reducing the risks of the patient dying from the particular circulatory problem, actually increase the risks of their dying from other causes (see Chapter 5).

Surgery?

Bypass and other interventions may be possible. These methods (see Chapter 5) help some but not all, and most are risky in themselves or have major drawbacks and few can do anything for brain function if this is the area of the body most affected.

Without question modern surgeons have evolved amazingly skilful techniques, including the following:

- Balloons are carefully threaded into an appropriate artery before being inflated in order to compress the concretions, thus making more space through which the blood can flow.
- Alternatively, instead of a balloon, a minute laser might be threaded along the artery to the place where there are concretions so that these can be 'blasted and burned' away.
- By means of the similar insertion of a minute, high-power drill or cutting instruments, the obstruction is partially chiselled or cut away.
- There is perhaps the choice of the grafting of veins from other regions of the body, or use of those donated by

animals or manufactured from special plastics, by which means the circulatory obstruction may be bypassed.

It is against the considerable known risks and variable and often very short-lived benefits – and of the limited success rate – which most of these methods offer, that we should measure the 'naturalness' or otherwise of a series of gentle infusions into the bloodstream of a synthetic amino acid, EDTA (ethylene-diamine-tetra-acetic acid).

This was initially thought to 'lock on' to the calcium cementing material which binds these concretions together and, by removing it from the scene, to allow the absorption of the rest of the material in the concretion (cholesterol, etc.). This somewhat simplistic picture of what happens has since been replaced by more recent research (described in Chapters 2, 3, 4 and 5), which explains a scientifically more acceptable concept of just how the improvements seen in chelation therapy actually do take place. It was originally thought that as well as leaching out calcium from atheromatous deposits, chelation therapy removed ionic calcium from cells in which it should not be present, thus reducing the chances of local arterial muscle spasms, increasing the free flow of tissue-enhancing, nutritive-rich blood. These benefits are certainly often apparent after chelation therapy, even if the precise mechanisms are not as simple as those which pioneer chelation therapists imagined.

What is known is that once atheromatous concretions lose the calcium which bind them, after a series of chelation infusions, the innate natural defence mechanisms of the body, aided by dietary and exercise methods where appropriate, safely take over the removal of the remaining debris which is impeding the blood flow.

Diet and exercise

For many, these can certainly offer help in the long term and should be included whatever else is done (drugs, surgery or chelation), but may not offer the speedy result needed. The exercise element may also be virtually impossible for anyone with intermittent claudication and out of the question, or at best extremely difficult, for someone with cerebral ischaemia or who has had a stroke.

Chelation therapy (combined where possible with dietary

and exercise strategies, and by means of mechanisms which will be discussed in later chapters) encourages the circulatory obstructions to be dissolved by the body's own efforts after the concrete binding the blocking material has been dissolved and removed.

Without doubt it would be better to use totally natural methods such as exercise and preventive nutritional approaches. But even if the person so affected were able to comply with the strenuous demands for compliance in such a programme there might not be time to do this before time ran out. Compromise as to what is totally 'natural' would seem to be a small price to pay if the method chosen is safe and is used as part of a comprehensive approach which not only attempts to restore normality to the circulation, but to ensure prevention of any recurrence.

Chapter 2

The chelation phenomenon: a natural biochemical process

In order to appreciate the truly remarkable potentials of chelation therapy it is necessary to examine briefly some of the chemical processes involved in the natural phenomena of chelation and free radical activity.

Our entire universe is made up of combinations of elements, the smallest unit of which is the atom. Each atom consists of a central nucleus, made up of *protons*, which is positively charged electrically. The number of protons in an atom determines what the element is. In the case of hydrogen, for example, there is just one proton, whereas carbon has 6 protons, sodium 11, calcium 20 and uranium 92.

Spinning around the central core of protons – in orbit, so to speak – are precisely the same number of negatively charged *electrons*, or, in the case of hydrogen, one electron. Electrons are much smaller than protons; by weight it actually takes 1835 electrons to equal one proton. Despite this imbalance in weight, the negative electrical charge of one electron is just as powerful as the positive electrical charge of one proton. Thus in a stable, electrically neutral atom, the electrical charge of the proton(s) is precisely in balance with that of the electron(s).

Electrons (much like people) have a natural tendency to find partners so that they can become paired. When this does not happen, as during radiation or certain chemical processes, a 'free radical', or a molecule (combination of atoms) with an unpaired electron may evolve (see below for more on these miniscule troublemakers).

Shells of electrons

The electrons which spin in orbit around the protons are

arranged in such a way as to form layers, or 'shells', each such shell being placed just a little further out than the previous one from the nucleus. The arrangement of electrons in each 'shell' or layer (in most atoms) is always the same, with two electrons in the inner shell and eight electrons in the next. In some instances atoms, instead of having their own complement of negatively charged electrons (which provide electrical balance and harmony to the positive electrical charge of the protons) actually share electrons with other atoms.

This is the way molecules (combinations of atoms) are formed, allowing, for example, the two gases hydrogen and oxygen to combine together to form water. Some atoms find that they can gain or lose anything from one to three electrons when necessary, thus turning themselves into *ions*. An ion is simply an atom or group of atoms which has lost or gained one or more of these orbiting electrons, for one of a number of reasons, and which has therefore in the process become capable of conducting electricity.

Technically, a *cation* is an ion with a positive electrical charge (this happens to an ion which has lost one or more electrons) and an *anion* is an ion which is negatively charged (this happens to an ion which has gained one or more electrons).

If we look at what happens when this process occurs between sodium and chlorine it should become clearer.

The process of crystallization of salt

The sodium atom (Na) has 11 protons at its core and therefore (since the number of protons equals the number of electrons) requires 11 electrons to balance it electrically.

As in other atoms the first 'shell' contains two electrons, and the second 'shell' eight. Simple arithmetic tells us that there is one more electron needing a home in the case of sodium, and this is found in orbit, on its own, in the third 'shell'. This so-called 'valency' electron is therefore available to attach itself easily to any passing atom which might be in need of an extra electron to complete its own electrical balance.

Chlorine (Cl) has 17 protons and 17 electrons. Again the 'shell' system demands two electrons in the inner layer, eight in the next and in chlorine an unbalanced seven electrons (remember eight is the ideal) are found in the outer 'shell'.

When sodium and chlorine are brought together, the 'odd' electron in sodium latches on to the seven in the chlorine to create a perfect 'shell' of eight electrons.

This process of combination creates a salt in which sodium and chlorine are bound together (in this case as table salt, NaCl) in a crystalline form. The sodium which has lost its free spinning electron (see above) is therefore now a positive ion, and this is expressed as Na^+, while the chlorine which has gained an electron has become a negative ion, expressed Cl^-. *Chelation* (pronounced *key-lay-shin*) is a natural interaction between an organic compound which has two or more 'available attachment points' (scientifically termed 'reactive sites') in its outer shell, with which it can link (co-ordinate) with a metal which happens to have two free electrons in its outer shell. It is axiomatic that a true chelation reaction has two or more such bonds or links. Together the organic compound (chelating agent) and the metal form a stable ring-like structure when they combine.

Chelation – a constant natural process

You (or indeed any living thing) could not survive without the constant benefits of chelation taking place, all the time, throughout your body. Digestion and assimilation of foods involves, for example, the ongoing process of chelation in which your body uses protein substances (amino acids) to chelate with minerals for transportation to their destinations, or in which blood cells latch on to, and thus acquire, iron. Indeed, haemoglobin is a chelate of iron (as is the enzyme catalase, which your body uses to 'switch off' the free radical activity of hydrogen peroxide). When you eat meat or green vegetables which contain iron, after the digestive process has released the iron from the food in which it is bound it has to be combined (chelated) with amino acids (protein fractions) so that it can be carried through the intestinal mucous membranes into the bloodstream.

However, if you drink tea at the same meal, the tannin in the tea will chelate with the iron (forming insoluble iron tannate) before it gets a chance to be absorbed, thus depriving your body of the iron. Should you, though, take some ascorbic acid (vitamin C) or eat vitamin C-rich food at the same meal as an iron-rich food, this will chelate with the iron and actually enhance and speed its absorption. The iron, once in the bloodstream, is released from the proteins with which it was chelated for transportation, so that it can recombine, in another chelating process, with blood chemicals to form transferrin which is then stored for later use.

Literally tens of thousands of body processes, involving the formation and function of enzymes, hormones and vitamins, constantly utilize similar chelation mechanisms. Similarly, countless examples of natural chelation are found in relation to plant life; for example, chlorophyll is a chelate of magnesium which has been processed during photosynthesis.

The word itself is derived from the Greek word (*chela*) which describes the prehensile claw of a scorpion or crab. This graphically evokes a picture of one substance grabbing or clutching and embracing another, as the chelation process takes place. *Chelation therapy* is the extension of this natural process to enable the removal from the body of undesirable ionic material by the infusion, or taking orally, of an organic compound which has suitable chelating properties.

One of the major substances being influenced during chelation therapy is calcium, as this process causes it to be removed from metastatic deposits while at the same time encouraging recalcification of bone (see description of atherosclerosis in Chapter 4). If calcium happens to be inappropriately present in certain body tissues (in a layer of plaque in the lining of an artery, or in excessive amounts on the surface of a joint in arthritis), it is of benefit, in health terms, to remove this, and chelation therapy safely allows exactly this to be done.

The number of electrons in a calcium atom is 20. This has an inner 'shell' of 2 electrons, two complete shells of 8 electrons each, and an outer shell of 2 'spare' electrons, which are therefore free to attach to a suitable molecule or atom which may be in need of 2 electrons (often called a 'complexing agent'). The symbol for the calcium cation, because of its two free electrons, is Ca^{++}.

In chelation therapy the 'suitable molecule' or 'complexing agent' with which this can link is a compound called EDTA (ethylene-diamine-tetra-acetic acid). Together EDTA and a metallic cation form a stable complex which can then be excreted from the system. The stability of this bond is vital to success in chelation therapy, for if there is a weak linkage other reactions breaking the bond could take place should the compound come into contact with suitable chemicals.

A chelating reaction which produces equilibrium, a strong and stable ring structure between the metal ion (calcium is a weakish link, iron, lead and copper are far stronger) and the chelating agent (such as EDTA), is effective in achieving the safe removal of the ion from the body.

When you use a water softener you are chelating calcium (and other minerals) out of the water. When you use a detergent in washing clothes or dishes, this chelates with minerals in the 'dirt', allowing the now soluble compounds to be washed away by water.

The brief survey of the early history of EDTA (see Chapter 3) will help to explain its tortuous route towards medical respectability as a means of removing unwanted mineral/metal substances. Before we look at the fascinating background to chelation therapy, one more facet of the imbalance which can result from unpaired electrons is worth examination.

Free radicals

Radiation is often described as ionizing radiation. This is because, by definition, it is able to dislodge individual electrons out of atoms and molecules, leaving unpaired electrons behind. This is one way in which free radicals are created. Some such molecules, with unpaired electrons, are extremely dangerous and can have very damaging effects on body tissues. Bleach (hydrogen peroxide), for example, does its damage to tissue (just think what it does to hair) through free radical action, as a deluge of these reactive entities chaotically bounce around, creating local havoc by grabbing on to any accessible electrons with which they come in contact (in this case from the hair itself).

Radiation is an example of how free radicals may be produced in the body when such an outside force acts on its cells. Perhaps more surprisingly there is almost continuous production of free radicals by some of the defending cells of the body. These are used as a means of destroying invading micro-organisms or cancer cells.

Since this is a natural process which is going on all the time in the body, there must exist control mechanisms to prevent undesirable effects from free radicals on healthy body cells, and this is the case when we are in good health.

Just as iron rusts, and an exposed apple or potato will turn brown when its surface meets the air, so do our bodies endure oxidation (ageing), for all of these are examples involving free radical activity. In the same way that the placing of lemon juice on an apple will stop it from turning brown by 'mopping up' the unpaired electrons, thanks to the antioxidant vitamin C in the juice, your body contains numerous antioxidant and free radical deactivating substances (specific enzymes, amino acids, vitamins, minerals, uric acid, etc.). The body can protect itself with these substances by quenching those free radicals which it produces itself, or which are created by radiation or from other sources. At least, it has these defensive substances to hand when it is well nourished. As we will see in Chapter 4, the processes which produce atherosclerosis have much to do with both free radical activity and with the accumulation of obstructive deposits, in which calcium acts as a cement or binding agent.

Free radical activity, now generally accepted to play a large part in the development of atherosclerosis as well as many other forms of damage to the body, including soft tissues, bone surfaces and nerve structures, is often associated with the presence in the body of heavy metals. Chelation can remove these metals before they do their damage. EDTA can also create the situation (low serum calcium, leading to parathyroid hormone production, leading to metastatic calcium removal, etc.) which starts the process of dissolution of atheromatous deposits which may be obstructing an artery in an area where free radical damage has already taken place. If such an approach is combined with nutritional patterns which encourage the intake of antioxidant substances (vitamins A, C, E, minerals such as selenium and zinc, etc.) an even better end result should be anticipated.

Dr Elmer Cranton's view

A leading American physician, Elmer Cranton, MD, states his expert view of the importance of using EDTA to counteract the free radical scourge (Cranton and Frackelton 1982):

EDTA can reduce the production of free radicals *by a million-fold*, for it is not possible for free radical pathology to be catalytically accelerated by metallic ions in the presence of EDTA. Traces of unbound metallic ions are necessary for uncontrolled proliferation of free radicals in living tissue and EDTA binds these ionic metal catalysts making them chemically inert and removing them from the body.

He continues:

> Two essential nutritional elements, iron and copper, are the most potent catalysts of lipid peroxidation [the degradation of fats by free radicals]. Catalytic iron and copper accumulate near phospholipid cell membranes, in joint fluid, and in cerebrospinal fluid with age and are released into tissue fluids following trauma or ischaemia [lack of oxygen supply due to circulatory inefficiency]. These unbound extracellular iron and copper ions have been shown to potentiate free radical tissue damage.

We will learn more about free radical activity, the damage caused by toxic heavy metals (and some apparently useful ones such as iron when in excess of requirements) and of the many protective functions of EDTA chelation therapy in relation to both free radical activity and heavy metal toxicity in later chapters, especially Chapter 5.

Chelation demonstration

Acetic acid is a mild chelator, far weaker than EDTA. Nevertheless, you can demonstrate for yourself the chelation process in action using the organic acid in vinegar (acetic acid).

Take an eggshell and place this in a bowl with some vinegar. Over a period of several days the eggshell will become increasingly thin, as the acetic acid progressively chelates the calcium out of the shell. Add more vinegar and the shell will eventually have all its calcium removed, leaving it in solution, bound (chelated) to the acetic acid.

It is just this process, much more efficiently performed, that EDTA achieves in the body when it acts on unwanted calcium deposits which are obstructing normal function.
   Remember that EDTA only does this with ionic, unbound, calcium and thus will not leach calcium out of

the normal bound sites such as the bones and teeth. By removing ionic, free calcium from the bloodstream, EDTA triggers parathyroid hormone to be released, which in turn compels the body to unbind metastatic calcium which may be cementing atheromatous plaque deposits in the blood vessels. In this way circulatory normality is encouraged.

Chapter 3

The history of EDTA

A half century of research in structural chemistry, much of it focusing on the ability of some amino acids to form constant, stable bonds with metal ions, preceded the rapid development in the 1930s and 1940s of a new range of compounds, initially applied to industrial, and then increasingly to medical, uses.

First in Germany and then in the USA, different methods were developed for the production of chelating substances for specific industrial use, such as the prevention of calcium in hard water from causing staining or other problems in textile printing. Citric acid was commonly used for this purpose until first a compound known as NTA, and then EDTA (ethylene-diamine-tetra-acetic acid), were developed and patented to do the job more efficiently.

During the Second World War research was carried out on sodium salts of EDTA in order to establish whether these would be useful as an antidote to poison gas. Earlier chelating compounds which had been used in this role, such as BAL (British anti-Lewisite), had proved effective when either externally applied or used systemically in neutralizing the arsenic in poison gas, but had themselves been found to be severely toxic in other ways.

A compound of sodium citrate was used in 1941 to chelate lead from the bodies of people poisoned by this heavy metal and later research established that EDTA contained a highly effective antidote to heavy metal toxicity (lead poisoning, for example), since it chelated just as well with lead as it did with calcium when it was infused into the bloodstream, and without any side-effects.

It was at Georgetown University that Dr Martin Rubin (who had studied under Frederick Bersworth, the major American pioneer researcher into EDTA) conducted the first research into the biological effects of EDTA on humans. These studies showed its effects on lowering calcium levels, although this had not been the objective of the work, which had focused on discovering its degree, or lack, of toxicity.

According to Dr Rubin, who was the chief researcher into EDTA's applications in treatment of humans at that time, a Dr Geschikter was the first to use an EDTA compound for treatment of a human. This work was also done at Georgetown University, using the chelating ability of EDTA to assist in the carrying into a patient of the heavy metal nickel – with which it had been chemically bound – in a vain attempt to treat an advanced tumour. There were sadly no benefits to the patient, but perhaps more importantly from the viewpoint of the benefits later seen with EDTA usage, there were no harmful effects either: *all* of the nickel-EDTA complex which was put into the patient was found to be excreted via the urine, unchanged.

It was in the early 1950s that EDTA was first used in the treatment of lead poisoning, with pleasantly surprising and often dramatically unexpected results. Workers in battery factories frequently developed lead poisoning, as did sailors in the US Navy who painted ships with lead-based paint. Intravenous infusions of EDTA successfully dealt with this problem, and indeed to this day the Food and Drug Administration (FDA) in the USA suggests EDTA chelation as the ideal method of treating not only lead poisoning but also as the emergency treatment for hypercalcaemia. It was found that there was often a marked improvement in the circulatory status of patients with chronic lead poisoning, who also had atherosclerotic (atheromatous deposits in the arteries) conditions and who were being treated by EDTA infusion.

It is worth considering that it is not just these naval personnel who are at risk from lead toxicity. The degree of general human body contamination with lead is now at five hundred times the level of people living just two hundred years ago. Lead has many toxic effects on the body, one of the more serious being its ability to prevent the body's natural control of free radical activity which itself can result in circulatory incompetence as well as many other problems.

Research studies by doctors such as Belknap, Butler, Spencer, Foreman, Clarke, Dudley, Bechtel, Jick, Surawicz, Boyle, Perry, Kitchell and many more (see References), published in the early and middle 1950s, all relate to aspects of the treatment of arterial disease using EDTA.

Since those pioneering days, techniques have evolved and have been improved for the successful application of EDTA chelation treatment of the disastrous effects not only of atherosclerosis, but also of circulatory obstructions to the brain in people with some forms of senility. Similar benefits have often been observed amongst those who have experienced cerebral accidents (stroke) or who are suffering from early gangrenous conditions. (The way in which EDTA is thought to work is discussed in chapter 5.) Relief and marked symptomatic improvement has been gained in countless instances of high blood pressure (essential hypertension) and problems involving peripheral circulation (Reynaud's disease) as well as occlusion of blood flow to the extremities (intermittent claudication).

A description of one of the earliest uses of EDTA in treating chronic cardiovascular disease was given in 1976 by Dr Norman Clarke, Sr, to the California Medical Association, in testimony before its Advisory Panel on Internal Medicine. He described his introduction to the process by research doctors (Drs Albert Boyle and Gordon Myers) at Wayne University, Detroit in 1953:

> They had had preliminary experience in treating two patients at University Hospital, Detroit, who had calcified mitral valves. The patients were almost completely incapacitated . . . the doctors were very pleased with the results [of chelation treatment] because they obtained very satisfactory return of cardiac function.

Dr Clarke spent many years investigating EDTA's usefulness in treating cardiovascular disease, and in his evidence stated: 'In the last 28 years of my experience with EDTA chelation I have given at least 100,000 to 120,000 infusions of EDTA and seen nobody harmed.'

He dramatically described the successful treatment of gangrene using EDTA, perfused directly into the site via a drip into the femoral artery, as well as this method's usefulness in cerebrovascular senility: 'After all these years, and with all that experience, I am just as certain as can be that EDTA chelation therapy is the best treatment that has ever been brought out for occlusive vascular disease.'

Other benefits from EDTA infusion

Just as the use of EDTA in treating lead poisoning revealed its ability to remove unwanted calcium, so additional benefits were discovered when circulatory conditions were being treated. Many patients with osteoarthritic and similar problems reported relief of symptoms and an improved range of movement in previously restricted joints. It seems that obstructive calcium deposits in these areas were also being removed during chelation treatment.

Other unexpected benefits which chelation therapy has produced in many patients include a reduction in the amount of insulin which diabetics require to maintain a stable condition, as well as marked improvements in many patients with kidney dysfunction (see also Chapter 6 on the potential danger to kidney function under certain conditions of wrong use of EDTA). More surprisingly, perhaps, a great deal of functional improvement in patients with Alzheimer's disease and Parkinson's disease is sometimes seen. Just how chelation could help in these states is not clear, apart from the unpredictable benefits of circulatory enhancement, and it may be that patients who appear to find relief from the symptoms of Alzheimer's and Parkinson's diseases might have had a faulty diagnosis, despite displaying all the classical signs associated with them.

New York studies on hyperactive children, using EDTA, have shown remarkable benefits, thought to relate to the removal of lead which may have accumulated in greater quantities in some of these children, due to their relative deficiency of major protective nutrients such as zinc and vitamin C, not uncommonly observed in such children.

As described in Chapter 5, there is also well-documented Swiss evidence of chelation therapy offering marked protection against the development of cancer as well as a suggestion that it could be useful in treating some forms of this disease.

Safety

The safety aspect of the use of EDTA in therapy has been phenomenal, with hardly any serious reactions being recorded amongst the host of seriously ill people to whom chelation therapy has been correctly applied. The commonest short-term side-effects, as well as precautions associated with EDTA usage, are discussed at length in Chapter 6.

By 1980 it was estimated by Bruce Halstead, MD, (Halstead 1979) that there had been over 2 million applications of EDTA therapy involving some 100 million infusions, with not a single fatality, in the USA alone. The most effective use of EDTA chelation therapy has, over the 30 years of its successful application, been consistently found to be related to those diseases in which heavy metal or calcium deposits are major factors.

Have there been double blind trials, the yardstick by which so much in medicine is judged? Hardly any, because, as Halstead states: 'It is impossible to administer EDTA blindly (i.e., so that neither the doctor nor the patient knows whether real EDTA or a substitute is being used), because it can be readily differentiated from an innocuous placebo by even one unacquainted with the compound.'

This is a major obstacle to its acceptance by mainstream medicine, but should not prevent those interested in its claims from examining the objective evidence. It should not require double-blind control studies to impress the observer with the possibility that people are actually getting better when severely ill people, with advanced circulatory problems, sometimes involving gangrene, show steady improvement in their functions, better muscular co-ordination, the disappearance of angina pain, increased ability to walk and work, restoration or improvement of brain function, better skin tone and more powerful arterial pulsations, along with the restoration of normal temperature in the extremities. This is particularly true in many patients who are slated to undergo bypass surgery, and this brings us close to one reason for orthodox medicine's rejection (in the main) of chelation's claims.

It might be that some of the simplistic theories as to how EDTA achieved its results may have prevented some scientists and physicians from taking it seriously or of investigating its potential. The current theories as to how calcium is encouraged to leave atheromatous deposits in blocked arteries have been well investigated by the proponents of chelation therapy and deserve to be seriously considered in view of the vast amount of illness attached to this area of human suffering and the remarkable results demonstrated by chelation physicians.

Bypass surgery and drug treatment of the conditions which

chelation so often effectively deals with are very big business indeed. In the USA alone, $4 billion is the current turnover per annum of the bypass industry. A lesser, but nevertheless enormous, sum is involved in medication for conditions which the relatively cheap (and now out of patent) substance EDTA can be shown to help (see Chapter 5 on bypass, etc.). Such vested interests should not be underestimated when it comes to the lengths to which they will go to try to discredit methods which threaten their stranglehold on the 'market'. Chelation therapy continues to grow, however, as public awareness and knowledge increases of this safe alternative to surgery and drugs, many of which are of questionable safety and value.

Chapter 4

Some causes of circulatory obstruction

The UK Health Education Council tells us that almost 40 per cent of all deaths of people between the ages of 35 and 74 arise as the result of stroke or heart attack. The majority of these crises result from circulatory restrictions or obstructions which are both preventable and treatable by chelation therapy.

Those problems arising from atherosclerosis are far and away the greatest health problem in industrialized societies. And as most people now know, cardiovascular and circulatory degenerative changes are to a very great extent preventable, since it is now well established that life-style practices and dietary habits contribute significantly towards their causation. So not only are most diseases which stem from circulatory degeneration largely preventable, in many instances they are at least partly reversible if causative factors are stopped and positive action taken.

However, the range of contributory factors is very wide indeed and no single method of prevention can possibly cover all of them, ranging as they do from the unavoidable – inherited tendencies, age and sex – to the (usually) controllable – smoking, dietary habits, stress coping abilities and exercise patterns. It has been demonstrated, in the Pritikin programme for example (Pritikin 1980), that much can be achieved through the application of self-applied dietary strategies, avoidance of known irritants (smoke, high-fat diet, etc.), combined with the application of aerobic exercise methods. Just how such methods can help, either on their own, or as part of a wider therapeutic approach – whether this involves drugs, surgery or chelation therapy – will become clearer once the known causes of circulatory obstruction are examined.

The value of chelation as an intervention strategy will also be seen to have marked advantages over many 'high-tech' approaches, in such conditions, once we comprehend that the entire arterial network is frequently damaged, requiring a method of treatment which addresses all 40,000 miles of it, rather than just local, isolated points of major blockage receiving attention.

The birth of an atherosclerotic lesion

There is no absolute consensus as to the causes of atherosclerosis, which probably means that all, or a number, of the theories are at least partially correct. It is therefore necessary to examine the most popular of these hypotheses.

In good health an artery (or arteriole) is far more than a simple plumbing conduit. As with so many parts of the body it also acts as a mini-factory, producing a large number of vital biochemical agents such as enzymes which act to protect it from damage which could arise via the action of a number of agencies (see below), such as excess fat in the bloodstream or other potential sources of free radical activity (see Chapter 2). The ability of such enzymes to perform their defensive and other functions depends on the abundant presence of co-factors (vitamins such as A, C, E, D) and an army of minerals and adequate protein sources for the amino and nucleic acids needed for regeneration and repair functions.

Vulnerability/susceptibility
Nutritional excellence is therefore the essential background to all other potential causes of arterial damage. If the nutritional status of the region is sound, the resulting abundant supply of defending substances will provide a powerful protective shield. Conversely, if nutrition is poor, vulnerability is greater and far fewer and lesser stress factors will be required before serious damage is caused.

We therefore need to keep in mind the underlying degree of (or lack of) nutritional soundness along with the list of constant influential factors (age, sex, inherited tendencies) in order to establish a base of vulnerability, susceptibility towards cardio-vascular disease.

In other words, we are not all starting from the same place, and noxious influences, whether these are toxic, dietary or life-style in origin, will affect one person quite differently from another because of this base-line susceptibility.

The shield will be weaker, the damage greater, the chances of recovery slighter, if nutrition is not dealt with as a primary and ongoing priority, whatever else is done in therapeutic terms. Basic guidance to the 'ideal' dietary pattern has been given by a variety of governmental and medical agencies over the past few years and this is discussed more fully in Chapter 8.

The free radical and the arterial wall

In Chapter 2 we discussed the way in which the hooligan-like behaviour of a free oxidizing radical might begin. Here we have, as the end-result of oxidation, highly reactive, electrically charged, molecular fragments with unpaired electrons in their outer shell, capable of grabbing on to other molecules in order to achieve the paired status to which all electrons aim. In capturing this new electron, forming a new chemical bond, the molecules from which the electrons have been taken become damaged and new free radicals are formed. Chain reactions can continue in this way until antioxidant substances (vitamins A, C, E, or enzymes such as catalase, or minerals such as selenium, or amino acids such as cysteine) quench the reaction. A single free radical can produce reactions involving thousands of damaged molecules, along with new free radicals, before the process burns itself out or is deactivated.

Why should such activity occur in the arteries?

Firstly, there is a plentiful supply of oxygen which fuels the free radical explosion. Secondly, there may be a relative lack of antioxidant substances (which is one reason why cardio-vascular disease is so much more evident where selenium or vitamins A or C are in poor nutritional supply). Thirdly, there may be present substances which easily generate free radical activity, such as fats and unbound (ionic) forms of metals such as iron and copper.

The fat connection

The walls of the cells of our bodies are made up to a large extent of lipids, which are extremely prone to peroxidation (rancidity), a process which involves massive free radical activity.

When food supplements of an oily nature (oil of evening

primrose, for example) are marketed, they are usually combined with antioxidant substances such as vitamin E or wheatgerm oil (which is rich in vitamin E) in order to damp down any free radical activity, allowing the product to remain stable for longer. A similar protective effect is constantly at work in the body itself if adequate antioxidant nutrients are present. In fact the most potent enzyme used by the body to protect its cells against lipid peroxidation is glutathione peroxidase, which is dependent on the antioxidant mineral selenium. If antioxidants such as these are lacking, or if other free radical generating factors are at work (alcohol, heavy metals or cigarette smoke, for example), a chain reaction of free radical activity can take place in the lipids of cell walls, severely damaging these.

It is now known that as we age, and certainly by middle age (45-55 approximately), a great many of the protective enzymes in the blood vessels and their walls are in rapid decline or are totally absent. Also apparent as we age is a build-up in the bloodstream of forms of cholesterol which increase the risks of cardiovascular disease, the low density lipoproteins (LDL). As we will discover in the next chapter, EDTA therapy has a remarkable normalizing effect on this dangerous build-up.

The seeds of later degeneration of arterial wall cells (and high levels of LDL-cholesterol) are often present in schoolchildren and certainly in most people in industrialized countries far earlier than middle age. According to major research in the USA and Europe, the first signs of degeneration of the arteries start early in childhood, often before schooling begins. Whether because of enzyme lack, metal toxicity or cholesterol (LDL) excess, free radical activity increases under such circumstances. The damage which takes place in cells during a free radical chain reaction goes beyond just the cell wall, often involving alterations to the genetic material of the cell, the DNA and RNA. If this happens, the way the cell reproduces itself will be altered, frequently leading, it is thought by many experts, to the beginning of atheromatous development (or of cancer, see Chapter 5).

A researcher in the USA, Earl Benditt, MD, first published in February 1977 (*Scientific American*) the theory of monoclonal proliferation. This suggested that damage to cells in the smooth muscles which lie below the inner lining of the artery are the initial site where damage occurs. It is here that we see the gradual evolution of atheromatous plaque which eventually erupts through the inner lining of the blood vessel. Whether the trigger for the original vessel-wall injury derives from free radical activity, excess cholesterol levels or from specific chemical or metal toxicity, or even from mechanical insult due perhaps to increased blood pressure, is not at issue (perhaps all or some of these, as well as other factors, interrelate in any given case and EDTA is able to normalize most of these).

Among EDTA chelation therapy's most important contributions to cardiovascular health are the ways in which it deactivates free radical activity and normalizes cholesterol excess. Indeed, some experts believe these to be even more important than its effects on calcium status. Elmer Cranton, MD, states (Cranton and Brecher 1984):

> If, as the newest research indicates, the free radical theory of degenerative disease is correct, then reversing free radical pathology would be the key to the treatment and prevention of such major age-related ailments as atherosclerosis. Specifically, EDTA reduces the rate of pathological free radical chemical reactions by a million-fold, below the level at which the body's defences can take over, and so provides time for free radical damage to be repaired by natural healing.

McDonagh and his colleagues (McDonagh, Rudolph and Cheraskin 1982b) report: 'Notwithstanding the general traditional consensus that serum cholesterol is physiologically different at different ages, our research shows that following EDTA plus supportive multivitamin/mineral supplementation *the serum cholesterol approaches about 200mg% (normal) in all age groups.*'

Some researchers see the development (after free radical activity) of atheromatous plaque as a defensive, protective reaction, whereas others do not agree with this concept. Whichever is correct, a sequence is commonly observed in which the inner lining (the intima which lies below the surface lining) of an artery becomes damaged, followed by the development of what seems to be an accumulation of debris at the site, consisting of a combination of connective tissue, elastin, collagen, cholesterol, polysaccharides and various protein fractions. If calcium also links up with such atheromatous deposits, a concrete-like state develops. Calcium, in its ionic form, is attracted to link and bind with the developing atheroma due to its electrical attraction to the substances in it.

It surely matters that largely preventable factors contribute to arterial damage, but it is to the processes which follow on from these developments, which ensure that the artery will become severely obstructed, that we need to turn.

To summarize, therefore, we see that a combination of low levels of antioxidant substances together with increased levels of free radical activity (for whatever reason and there are many possible, including excess presence of forms of cholesterol (LDL) and heavy metal imbalances), results in damage to cells deep within the arterial walls. This is usually followed or accompanied by the evolution of thickening of the arterial walls and the development of atheromatous changes.

Where does calcium come into the picture?

We need to look briefly at the enormous subject of calcium and its functions, its balance and imbalance in the blood vessels and bloodstream, along with calcium's link with diet, exercise, the ageing process, free radical damage and subsequent athero-sclerosis.

Calcium is one of the most important elements in the body and, together with magnesium, is vital for cardiovascular health. In the main calcium is used by the body extracellularly (along with sodium), as opposed to potassium, magnesium and zinc which are largely found intracellularly.

Ninety-nine per cent of all calcium in the body is found bound to phosphorus in bones and teeth. However, more important to us is the ionic form of calcium which is found in the body. Around 60 per cent of all the calcium in the bloodstream is in the ionic form (Ca^{++}) where its degree of concentration ranges from 9 to 11 milligrams per 100 millilitres of serum. This ionic calcium is very important in the body economy, being instantly available for use chemically, especially in relation to coagulation of blood, as well as heart, muscle and nerve function and the permeability of cell membranes.

The distribution of calcium in the body in good health and disease varies greatly. Under ideal conditions, largely controlled by the activity of the parathyroid hormone, calcium levels are as follows:

- The bulk of stored stable calcium in the body is approximately 1 kilo in the bones and teeth.

- Between 2 and 4 grams of the calcium in the bones is in the ionic form which is 'exchangeable' with the amount of calcium 'transported' daily, into and out of bone, commonly around 3 grams.
- This interchange is between bone and the calcium held extracellularly (around 1-1.5 grams) and intracellularly (4-10 grams), in the plasma (less than .5 gram) and in interstitial fluids (under 1 gram).

Under certain circumstances, as in osteoporosis, deposition of calcium takes place around joints (soft tissues) and in arteries. Such abnormal calcium deposits are known as metastatic or dystrophic deposits, some of which contain ionic calcium.

Parathyroid hormone (which is markedly influenced by the degree of acidity of the blood, and production of which is stimulated by EDTA infusion – see below), as well as calcitonin and vitamin D3, control and regulate calcium flux between extracellular and intracellular calcium, so vital in cellular function as well as in those enzyme systems which influence muscle contractility, nerve transmission and some hormone activities.

Ionic pump
The transfer of substances including water across cell membranes involves the activity of ionic forms of many minerals including sodium, potassium, magnesium and calcium. It is in the mitochondria of cells that intracellular calcium is found, most usually bound as a phosphate rather than in ionic (free) form.

In an adult, 20 per cent of the total bone calcium is re-absorbed and replaced each year, in normal health, but when replacement is inadequate, serious problems arise. Thus, apart from its role in providing structural integrity to the skeleton and teeth, calcium is also of vital importance in the processes of growth and development, and the maintenance of health, and yet it presents us with an apparent paradox.

It is now known that, if overall nutrient imbalances exist, a high-protein diet is capable of speeding up the removal of calcium from bones and of contributing to osteoporosis. This has occurred in many millions of women in Europe, America and other industrialized nations of the world. Post-menopausal women in particular are thus vulnerable to easily fractured bones, after even slight injury. Many factors contribute towards this, but one of the major elements appears to be an imbalance in the ratio of calcium-to-phosphorus in the diet. Phosphorus is found in very large quantities in meat and in most other proteins as well as in carbonated drinks.

Paleolithic evidence
Stone-age man ate abundant meat (in excess of 700 grams daily), as do current hunter gatherers, and yet their bone structures remained, and remain, sound into old age.

This is a paradox.

The complex process which occurs when a high-protein diet is consumed may be linked to a high degree of acidity in the body. Increased acidity increases parathyroid hormone production and a consequence of this is additional resorption of calcium from bone into the bloodstream. If additional vitamin D is also present in the body this progression may be limited (and the body of course makes vitamin D when sufficient sunlight is available to it).

Another factor which appears to prevent decalcification is exercise. It is possible that these two protective factors, sunshine and exercise, which were abundantly available to stone-age man, may account for the difference noted in the effect of a high-protein diet in those people, as opposed to such a diet in a sedentary individual, where decalcification is more common.

We are obliged to ask therefore why, if an EDTA infusion stimulates parathormone production and subsequent calcium withdrawal from bone (as well as from pathological deposits in atheromatous plaque, etc.), this does not lead to osteoporosis?

Bruce Halstead (1979) answers this as follows:

Physicians having extensive clinical experience with EDTA in the treatment of atherosclerosis have generally observed that the bone structure improves with the administration of EDTA. The explanation of the apparent paradox is to be found in the role parathormone plays in relationship to osteoblastic function. When EDTA is administered intravenously into the body there is a rapid complexing of ionic serum calcium and excretion of calcium EDTA through the renal tubules. This causes a drop in circulating calcium and a stimulation of parathormone production . . . which results in withdrawal of ionic calcium from metastatic deposits *and also increases the conversion of preosteoblasts to osteoblasts . . .* leading to an increase in total collagen synthesis or new bone formation . . . This basic biochemical mechanism of bone metabolism has been well documented experimentally and provides a reasonable explanation as to why EDTA generally improves bone structure rather than producing osteoporosis clinically.

Other factors

Increased sugar in the blood causes a decrease in the circulation of vitamin D, which if present helps to neutralize the sequence of events described:

High protein = high acidity levels in the blood = high parathyroid hormone = low levels of calcium in the blood = decalcification.

(Recall that if EDTA infusion is the cause of this sequence the final result is not decalcification of bone, only of metastatic deposits.)

Interestingly there is a family of plants which contain a material which acts very much like vitamin D in protecting against bone decalcification where blood acidity stimulates decalcification. This is the solanaceous family of plants, which includes tomatoes, potatoes, green peppers and aubergine.

One of the most critical elements in the whole equation of balances and imbalances involved in this highly complex scenario relates to the ratio between calcium and phosphorus in the diet. It has been found that the demineralization of bones ceases, and actually reverses (bone begins to remineralize) when the ratio of calcium to phosphorus is 1 (that is, one part of calcium for every one part of phosphorus in the diet: $1 \div 1 = 1$). Commonly the diet in Western society achieves a ratio of less than 0.5 parts of calcium to each part of phosphorus ($\frac{1}{2} \div 1 = \frac{1}{2}$).

Stated simply this means that whilst experimentally it can be shown that a high-protein diet increases calcium excretion and bone loss, this does not appear to be nearly so likely when the overall diet is balanced, even though there is a high protein intake.

Some experiments which appeared to implicate a high-protein diet as the major cause of calcium loss have been shown to be seriously flawed, as the type of protein used was a concentrated, often liquid, protein, bearing little resemblance to the forms of protein normally eaten. Such concentrated purified proteins are the types often used in crash slimming programmes as well as in some emergency refeeding programmes, where malnutrition exists.

Phosphorus itself is now seen to be useful and necessary in achieving a balance against the acid side-effects of a high-protein diet. So phosphorus and calcium, in balance, produce the situation in which a sound bone structure can be achieved even where there is a high meat intake. A high vegetable content in the diet ensures lowered acidity as well as calcium replenishment.

Calcium from vegetables

Some of the best sources of calcium are from green leafy vegetables such as dandelion greens, mustard greens, turnip and beet tops, watercress, broccoli and kale.

Other protective factors

The other important elements in maintaining healthy nerve and bone structures include exercise and daylight. Exercise taken in an environment in which light is available is therefore important. Direct sunlight is not important as even indirect daylight has beneficial effects in the production of vitamin D.

Thus there is no real paradox: a high-protein diet is not going to result in decalcification unless there is an imbalance between calcium and phosophorus and unless acidity clearly outweighs alkalinity. Neither of these is likely if sound eating patterns are followed, and even less likely if exercise and light are obtained in liberal quantities.

The start of arteriosclerosis and atherosclerosis

We have seen a variety of often interacting influences on calcium status in the body. If for any reason calcium levels in the blood are too low, the action of parathyroid hormone withdraws ionic calcium from other (often metastatic) sources to meet this imbalance. If EDTA is the cause of the reduction in ionic calcium levels in the blood, then (as explained by Bruce Halstead above) osteoblasts are stimulated to start the process of bone calcification. However, if calcium levels increase in the bloodstream (as they would if withdrawn from bone as in osteoporosis), calcitonin produced by the thyroid lowers it, often causing it to be deposited in metastatic forms. In good health, around one gram of calcium should be absorbed from the intestines daily, but if far more calcium is ingested, or the intake of magnesium is low, excess calcium will either be excreted via the kidneys or added to the dystrophic depositions in soft tissues (arteries, etc.). If this occurs in arteries it may be in one of two forms. There might be localized, discrete deposits which show up well as radiopaque shadows on X-ray; or there may be a more generalized, diffuse deposition in which calcium is secreted in the previously elastic fibres of the arteries. Generalized calcification of arteries is not radiopaque until it is well advanced.

Age

With passing time multifaceted influences (diet, life-style, toxic exposure, stress, lack of exercise, etc.), interacting with the normal ageing process may lead to one or other of these forms of arterial degeneration. As the general calcification described above proceeds, there is a gradual lessening of the ability for oxygen and nutrients to be transported and absorbed, with consequent deterioration of the status of the tissues being fed. This is arteriosclerosis and it may impair circulation to any body part, including the brain, leading in such a case to impaired ability to concentrate, remember or think, or to transient dizziness; hearing and sight might be impaired; tinnitus might develop; the extremities, especially the legs, might feel colder or be subject to cramp; the heart muscle itself might become starved of oxygen and nutrients, developing the symptoms of angina; the ageing process may be seen to be advanced steadily, and as it progresses, in time muscular spasm may completely shut down one or other of the arterial channels of circulation.

In atherosclerosis, where more localized deposits of atheromatous material form on the artery wall, there is an inevitable turbulence and increased pressure of the flow of blood at that point. The atheromatous deposit could continue to increase in size until it obstructed the artery or there is always the chance of a fragment of such a plaque deposit breaking away and being carried to a point too narrow for its passage, completely or partially blocking this. A cerebral accident or coronary infarct would then have occurred.

Mineralization by ionic calcium of plaque, forming around localized lesions, seems to have attracted a great deal of medical attention. Not only do these contain various forms of calcium, such as carbonate apatite – $Ca_{10}(Po_4)_6CO_3$, but also concretions containing barium, strontium or lead. However, we should not underestimate the progressive damage resulting from generalized arterial calcification with its slowly progressive loss of elasticity and circulatory capacity.

Both forms of arterial degeneration involve ionic calcium to some extent and both are amenable to chelation therapy's ability to start the process by which calcium and other metals are removed from such concretions, initiating (relative) normalization.

It was never the intention of this chapter to explore fully all possible causes of atherosclerosis (other more comprehensive texts exist which do this perfectly adequately – see Further Reading), but rather to point to the need in many such conditions to deal with both ongoing contributory causes of calcium imbalance/cardiovascular dysfunction (acid/alkaline imbalance, calcium/phosphorus imbalance, calcium/magnesium imbalance, high fat intake, low vegetable/complex carbohydrate intake, etc.), as well as having a strong image of the need that may exist for a method simultaneously (together with the correction of the imbalances mentioned) to remove deposits of metastatic calcification.

The menstruation–hysterectomy–iron connection

Dr Elmer Cranton (Cranton and Frackelton 1982) explains a fundamental and somewhat revolutionary concept of atherosclerosis development when he reminds us of another slant to chelation therapy using not EDTA but deferoxamine: 'This has been shown to improve cardiac function in patients with increased iron stores ... as well as reducing inflammatory responses in animal experiments.' EDTA also has a strong affinity for iron and Cranton suggests that the individual's iron status is a critical element in the background to atherosclerosis development.

Women of menstrual age are four times less likely to develop such arterial changes as men of the same age. Also, men accumulate iron in the blood (serum ferritin) at precisely four times the rate of pre-menopausal women and it is no coincidence that these two factors have the same degree of measurable numerical similarity (four times the iron and four times the arterial damage), since iron is a potent catalyst of lipid peroxidation with all its potentially devastating circulatory repercussions.

It could be argued that this protection from atherosclerosis is all down to hormonal influences present in young women and not men. But this is not so, says Cranton, as he provides us with the clinching link between iron and the damage discussed above.

When women are studied following hysterectomy, it is observed that there is an immediate rise in their iron levels to equal that of men of the same age and *their susceptibility to atherosclerotic changes also rises to that of men* (Cranton and Brecher 'Bypassing Bypass'). These changes after removal of the womb (thereby stopping menstruation) are seen whether the ovaries (which produce oestrogen) are retained or not. Clearly, the monthly blood loss is protective and Cranton suggests that a good way for men and post-menopausal women to reduce the risk of atherosclerosis would be to become regular blood donors.

Chelation therapy of course offers another way of reducing excessive iron levels. We have seen above that calcium in its ionic form is reasonably easily chelated by EDTA. However, calcium is not high on the list of substances to which EDTA is most attracted. In descending order, the stability of a chelation link between EDTA and various metals (at normal levels of acidity of the blood) is as follows:

Chromium^2 – iron^3 – mercury^2 – copper^2 – lead^2 – zinc^2 – cadmium^2 – cobalt^2 – aluminium^3 – iron^2 – manganese^2 – calcium^2 – magnesium^2.

How toxic metals such as lead interfere with protection

Elmer Cranton and James Frackelton (1982) explain the ways in which lead toxicity can prevent the body from doing its natural protective work against free radical activity: 'Lead reacts vigorously with sulfur-containing glutathione peroxidase (a major antioxidant enzyme used by the body against free radicals) and prevents it reacting with free radicals.' They also explain how reduced glutathione further harms the body by preventing the recycling of antioxidant (protective) vitamins such as E and C and other enzymes: 'Lead therefore cripples the free radical protective activity of that entire array of antioxidants.'

And EDTA was developed precisely to remove lead from the system.

These insights into how circulatory damage occurs and the ways in which EDTA helps prevent or repair such happenings, as explained by experts in the field of chelation, should help us understand the irrelevance of trying to state precisely *how* and *why* EDTA therapy works so well in any given case. What *is* important is its proven value and relative safety.

Chapter 5

EDTA – how it works and what it does

Current medical crisis care in dealing with many acute manifestations of cardiovascular and circulatory disease, such as coronary thrombosis and cerebrovascular accidents, is superbly efficient and often surprisingly successful at saving life (surprising considering the state of the patients, that is).

Heroic intervention, high-technology diagnostic and monitoring methods, skilled nursing, intensive and complex medication and, where appropriate, surgery of sometimes mind-boggling complexity, all add up to a magnificent refinement of those many skills required for the saving of life after a sudden infarct, thrombosis or embolism, as well as other major causes of emergency circulatory mayhem.

But . . .

There is a darker side to the brilliant progress exemplified by such medical techniques, relating to an apparent lack of awareness of, or interest in, safer alternative treatment methods for dealing with pre-crisis conditions. Among these relatively inexpensive and safe preventive measures must be numbered chelation therapy. (It is also useful in treatment of coronary thrombosis – see below.)

Many of the drugs used by conventional medicine for prevention and treatment of such conditions do not address causes but rather tamper with symptoms (for example, drugs which lower blood pressure, while ignoring the causes of its elevation, or which interfere with calcium uptake without dealing with the long-term effect of residual calcification, or drugs which attempt to reduce heightened cholesterol levels, proving themselves successful at this task but leading to a higher mortality rate from other causes than were nothing done at all). Most such drugs create at least as many problems as they solve (compare this with the results of EDTA treatment on cholesterol as described below).

There is also strong evidence of the overuse of surgical methods, such as bypass surgery; indeed, a recent US survey indicated that almost half of bypass operations were not essential, even though this survey took orthodox criteria as to what was 'essential' as the yardstick.

And what about transplants? The concentration of surgical experts and their back-up teams with high-tech, spectacular, surgical methods (such as are employed in transplant surgery) benefit very few (albeit often amazingly so), while depriving or delaying care for many more through such allocation of scarce resources.

In the USA, where chelation now has a 30-year track record, it might be expected that insurance companies would be supportive of chelation therapy as a cheaper alternative to bypass surgery. And yet this not yet so. A recent legal action, brought by a patient against his insurance company (for refusing to pay his expenses for highly successful chelation treatment) led to some pertinent comments from the judge trying the case. The case was heard in Lorain County, Ohio, where the judge, George Ferguson, ordered Aetna Insurance to pay the chelation expenses, stating in his judgement:

> It is interesting to note that the Defendant (insurance company) would presumably pay for very expensive bypass surgery where there have been 4000 deaths in 300,000 cases, but is refusing to pay for chelation therapy where there have been approximately 20 deaths in 300,000 cases. Insurance companies are repeatedly urging second opinions where surgery is recommended. The Plaintiff was advised to have surgery on June 2 1987, at Elyria Memorial Hospital. Plaintiff obtained a second opinion from a duly licensed physician, followed the second physician's advice (chelation therapy), is alive today and saved the insurance company the expensive coronary bypass surgical operation. (*Day vs. Aetna Life Insurance Company, 87CVI2710, Elyria Municipal Court, Lorain County, Ohio, 1988*)

The complexities of prejudice, ignorance of alternatives, and in some cases outright vested commercial interest, are all sometimes involved in the antagonism of many medical practitioners to chelation therapy. Nevertheless, hundreds of physicians support its simpler and safer approaches to degenerative cardiovascular conditions, and its safety record is evident to all who wish to investigate it.

Just what does EDTA do when it is infused? In order to appreciate its activities we need to return to cellular metabolism for a short while.

Reducing free radical activity

Body cells contain miniature factories in which complex biochemical processes are continuously underway with raw materials being turned into energy and protein compounds. Within the cell there exist internal transportation mechanisms and also the means for the transfer of raw materials into the cell, as well as of processed products and wastes out of it. These precise and dynamic functions, however, many of which depend upon complex enzyme activity, are vulnerable should the materials which surround the cell become damaged.

The intracellular membrane which surrounds the cell is far from being a mere envelope, but is involved in important organizational functions, including the control of what passes through it. The active cell membrane is itself made up of lipids (and cholesterol), proteins and water. Should free radical activity take place in its vicinity, destructive effects occur, producing lipid peroxidation (this is what happens when fats become rancid). When this occurs the functioning of cell 'factories' would be either severely disorganized or put out of action, the organizational enzymes could be lost, the distribution of raw material and finished manufactured products and energy disorganized, and a process started of local tissue degeneration.

This is the picture of what happens when atherosclerosis begins in an artery wall. Much lipid peroxidation activity involves the presence of metal ions such as iron, copper or calcium and it is these which EDTA so effectively locks onto, preventing their destructive influence from operating.

Research over the past 30 years has confirmed this benefit from EDTA (e.g. Barber and Bernheim). Of course, this protective influence would be much enhanced were there an appreciable presence of antioxidant nutrients such as vitamins C and E, selenium, and amino acid complexes such as glutathione peroxidase, which not only mop up free radical activity but also assist in building up cell membrane stability.

Cell energy production

Within each cell there reside up to 2500 miniature energy producing factories, the mitochondria. One of the main functions of each mitochondria is to translate inorganic phosphate (ADP), sugar (glucose) and oxygen into adenosine triphosphate (ATP), the universal form of energy used by the body. This energy producing activity of the mitochondria involves a series of intricate, complex and vital biochemical processes dependent on vast numbers of enzymes (estimates vary from between 500 to 10,000 complete sets of oxidative enzymes in each mitochondria) which are themselves dependent upon dozens of nutrient factors and co-factors.

If calcium is abnormally deposited in arterial walls this inhibits some enzyme activity and negatively influences ATP (energy) production. If through free radical activity, or through any other disturbing influences on normal energy production or transfer by damaged mitochondria, cells can become energy starved, they tend then to become more acidic. This happens for a multitude of reasons: it may be to do with ageing or to calcium/magnesium ratios becoming unbalanced, due to free radical activity, local toxicity, oxygen deficit, nutritional imbalance, etc. Elmer Cranton, MD, reminds us that 'EDTA increases the efficiency of mitochondrial oxidative phosphorylation (energy production) quite independently of any effect on arterial blood supply' and let us not forget his statement that EDTA can reduce the production of free radicals by a million-fold.

Cells which have become energy starved and more acidic for whatever reason start to attract calcium ions, drawing them into the cell, further blocking energy production. An increase in calcium inside cells, accompanied by reduced oxygen and lower energy manufacture and availability, is a typical picture found in degenerative cardiovascular conditions. It is also a prescription for the muscles which surround the arteries to go into spasm. This is the reason for the use of calcium channel blocker drugs, which may be effective in blocking calcium uptake by muscle cells but do nothing about the underlying condition.

Morton Walker and Garry Gordon (1982) have discussed calcium channel-blocking drugs:

> Calcium channel blockers are not as efficient in permanently restoring heart health as is EDTA chelation therapy, but even these calcium antagonists are clearly better, as a coronary medical programme, than open heart surgery. They inhibit the excessive accumulation of calcium in the heart cells and allow ATP production. Additionally, if you are the patient in heart spasm, you can help avoid death of the starved portion of your heart muscle. You will not show the elevated enzymes (CPK, LDH, SCOT and others) that your doctor measures in your blood test each day to see how many heart cells have really died and released their enzymes. An actual heart attack will be avoided . . . you will usually be able to go home from hospital the next day by having calcium channel-blocking agents and/or chelation therapy.

Elmer Cranton and Arline Brecher (1984) describe some of the stages involved:

> Impairment of the calcium/magnesium pump allows more ionized calcium to enter the cell, activating an enzyme that leads to the production of prostaglandin related leukotrienes, a chemical process which releases free radicals. When excessively stimulated by leukotrienes, white blood cells run amok and initiate free radical production, which causes increasing inflammatory damage to healthy tissues. Small blood vessels dilate, causing swelling, oedema, and leakage of red blood cells and platelets through blood vessel walls which result in microthrombi (microscopic clots). Some red blood cells then haemolyse releasing free copper and iron, which in turn catalyse an increase of free radical destruction to lipid membranes in the vicinity of a million-fold, triggering another vicious cycle.

This process is compounded by the presence of additional vitamin D and cholesterol because free radical activity helps to convert cholesterol into substances with vitamin D activity, resulting in plaque (in which cholesterol is usually bound) attracting calcium, thus cementing the material.

EDTA infusion, which has the ability to remove metal ions, stops or slows metals which are significant causes of free radical production. In removing metals, local toxicity is reduced and enzyme production and function improves. We should not underestimate the role of toxic metal ions in the body, whether these are of lead, mercury, cadmium, copper, iron or aluminium. Once these have been chelated by EDTA and removed from their deposition sites, free radical activity and consequent disruption of metabolic function is largely prevented. Once this has happened normal enzyme function resumes.

A further well-established effect of EDTA infusion involves the improvement of cell membrane integrity and consequent protection of mitochondria activity. If this is happening in the heart muscle itself, such improvement in cell function (enhanced energy production via enhanced mitochondria activity) often allows a strong chance of salvaging and regenerating previously damaged muscle function, with benefits to the heart and therefore the body as a whole.

Research by Dr C Gallagher as long ago as 1960 (Gallagher, 1960) showed that the natural ageing of the mitochondria could be counteracted by use of EDTA.

Reducing blood 'stickiness'

Not only does EDTA remove circulating ionic calcium from the blood, but it also acts directly on improving the function of blood platelets. These (which contain granules, lysosomes, mitochondria and glucose), along with red and white blood cells (erythrocytes and leucocytes), make up much of the 'solid' material suspended in the blood plasma which itself is made up of a complex of protein-based substances including fibrinogen, albumin and globulin, as well as carrying in solution salts, hormones and a variety of metabolic products and wastes.

Platelets have as a major function the role of initiating repair of any damaged internal lining in blood vessels. This they accomplish, under the direction of prostaglandin hormones called prostacyclin (which discourages clotting and reduces muscle spasm) and thromboxane (which encourages muscle spasm and the stickiness of blood), firstly by adhering to the damaged surface, gradually covering the region of injury, while at the same time reducing the danger of haemorrhage by encouraging a degree of coagulation of the blood. As all this happens, the shape of the platelets alters from a disc shape to a more irregular form, with radiating filaments known as pseudopodia extending from them as well as developing inside them. These protective functions of platelets are therefore life-enhancing. But, should the process of organization of clots (coagulation) take place in a cerebral artery the consequences could well be life-threatening and would certainly pose a hazard until it resolved.

Just how EDTA reduces these dangers is not clear, but it does. The reduction, after use of EDTA, in the tendency to over-coagulation is thought by some to relate to the way EDTA removes ionic calcium from the membrane of the platelet. Or it may be that a more healthy, balanced production of the prostaglandins which control platelet function and activity are influenced by the way EDTA inhibits lipid peroxidation, since prostaglandins are the product of lipids which can be severely damaged by free radical activity.

Normalizing abnormal cholesterol and high density lipoprotein (HDL) levels

As we age there is an increasing tendency for our blood-cholesterol levels to rise. High blood cholesterol was for many years used alone as a marker of increased risk of cardiovascular disease. The fashion for blaming all cholesterol has only partly been reduced in the public mind through education, but medical practitioners now know that it is only some forms of cholesterol which pose a real threat – the low density forms (LDL). Indeed, the ratio between total cholesterol and HDL (high density lipoprotein — the beneficial form) is now used as a clear indication of relative safety or danger, in terms of being a predictor of cardiovascular disease.

In a series of simple but effective experiments, McDonagh, Rudolph and Cheraskin (1982b) have shown that EDTA infusion has a markedly beneficial effect on this potentially serious problem.

The effects on over 200 patients with varying levels of HDL-cholesterol measurements were quite dramatic. Those who initially showed *low* levels of HDL rose to normal levels; those with normal levels remained unaltered, and those with *high* levels of LDL (dangerous) dropped to normal ranges after EDTA-chelation therapy (supported with vitamin and mineral supplementation).

Thus we see a homoeostatic (balancing, normalizing) effect

after the use of EDTA, since it supported a return towards normal HDL-cholesterol levels, whether the initial abnormality was high or low.

How long before such change starts to be significant?

This same team of researchers, working in a private practice setting, found that: '... there appears to be a significant reduction in serum cholesterol within the first month or so (range of 12-36 days) of treatment with EDTA ... in private practice environment, irrespective of the age or sex of the patient.' Excitingly, it was found that: '... those with the highest initial cholesterol scores decreased about twice as much as those with the lower first score (approximately 17 per cent as against 9 per cent).'

With regard to the ratios between total cholesterol and HDL, these homoeostatic effects were measured as follows:

The 'normal' balance between total cholesterol and HDL is considered to be a ratio of 4.5:1. The McDonagh, Rudolph and Cheraskin team found that those with 'relatively low ratios (under 4.0) tended to rise, while those with relatively high ratios (over 5.0) tended to decline, and those in the range 4.0-4.9 tended to remain unchanged.'

This important research is deserving of far wider awareness and application since cardiovascular disease is the number one killer and these risk factors are demonstrably easy and safe to control or normalize (by EDTA, diet and life-style changes).

Removal of calcium from plaque

In Chapter 4 we looked at some of the ways in which cardio-vascular disease developed. Once a localized area of plaque has accumulated in an artery, following some degree of local irritation and subsequent repair (which the plaque represents to a large extent), there exists a strong case for trying to remove any calcium in the plaque in order to prevent its inevitable build-up towards this becoming a complete obstruction. It is the loosely bound calcium in the plaque, held by an electrostatic charge, which prevents the body from dissolving it. When EDTA is infused it mops up the ionic (free) calcium in the blood serum, triggering release of parathormone. This produces a demand for calcium in the blood and this is first mobilized from the calcium deposited in metastatic sites (plaque, soft tissue deposits, etc.), thus allowing the process of resorption of the plaque material and restoration of normal arterial status.

However, this does not happen quickly. It is only by repetitive, very slow infusions of EDTA that the process takes place safely.

Does this not damage bone and tooth structure?

On the contrary, the status of bone is enhanced after a series of EDTA chelation infusions. This is directly related to the influence of parathyroid hormone. After EDTA infusion there is a rapid removal of ionic calcium from the bloodstream (the EDTA/calcium complex is excreted via the kidneys). The resulting drop in circulating calcium stimulates parathyroid hormone production which results in the removal of ionic calcium from metastatic deposits (such as occur in plaque). At the same time a phenomenon occurs in response to para-thormone, described by Doctors Rasmussen and Bordier (1974), in which preosteoblasts are converted into osteoblasts.

Since osteoblasts are the cells which form bone, building the osseous matrix of the skeleton, new bone formation is thus encouraged. This is often confirmed by X-ray examination of bone before and after a series of chelation infusions.

According to Cranton and Brecher (1984):

> Pulsed intermittent parathormone stimulation, produced by each chelation (treatment) is known to cause a lasting effect on osteoblasts of approximately three months' duration. This is a proven effect of EDTA, and one that makes perfect sense, for it provides a hypothetical explanation for the three month waiting period for complete benefit following a series of intravenous EDTA therapy infusions.

Walker and Gordon (1982) suggest that:

> Soft tissue pathological calcium in plaques or arterial cells continues to diminish in order to meet the need caused by the increased bone uptake of calcium. The therapeutic cycle continues long after a series of chelation treatment has been completed and patients continue to improve all this time.

They describe the work of Dr Carlos Lamar who explained his findings on this topic at the fourteenth annual meeting of the American College of Angiology in 1968. Dr Lamar had demon-strated that as calcification of the blood vessels decreased so did simultaneous recalcification take place of previously osteoporotic vertebral and femoral bones. Similarly, metastatic calcium deposits in arthritic joints was often seen by Dr Lamar to decrease. In such cases deformity often remained but symptoms of pain and immobility were reduced or absent after chelation therapy. Walker and Gordon remind us, however, that chelation itself is not the whole answer: 'Hardened arteries get softer and softened bones get harder following proper EDTA chelation therapy – *where appropriate mineral supplementation with zinc, magnesium and other minerals is being given, dietary calcium/phosphorus ratio is balanced and active exercise undertaken.'* [original italics]

The cancer connection

By now the concept of free radical damage resulting in tissue damage and consequent deterioration of circulatory function should be quite familiar. It is perhaps less apparent that free radical damage is frequently the trigger which leads to malignant changes in previously normal cells. Just as the first benefits to circulation of EDTA chelation therapy were discovered during treatment of heavy metal poisoning, so was the way in which this same treatment could help prevent, and indeed treat, cancer discovered.

Writing in a Swiss medical journal in 1976, Dr W Blumen described the strange but potentially very important discovery. In the late 1950s a group of residents of Zurich who lived adjacent to a major traffic route were treated for contamination by lead with EDTA chelation under the auspices of the Zurich Board of Health. These people had all inhaled large amounts of lead-laden fumes and were suffering from a range of symptoms identified as being related to lead poisoning, including stomach-ache, fatigue, headache, digestive symptoms, etc. Lead deposits were found to be present in their gum tissues and specific changes were found in their urine, linking their condition with high lead levels.

Some years later, in the early 1970s, people living in the same area were being investigated for the incidence of cancer, in an attempt to link the pollution with a higher cancer rate than average. This link was easily established as fully 11 per cent of the residents of the road had died of cancer over the period 1959 to 1972, a rate some 900 per cent above that expected when compared with people living in the same community but not directly affected by lead pollution. The forms of cancer most commonly related involved the lungs, colon, stomach, breast and ovary.

But what of the people previously treated with EDTA back in 1959?

Only one of the 47 people in that group had developed cancer. The cancer rate in people in the contaminated area who had not received EDTA was 600 per cent above that of the group who had had chelation.

Far and away the best protection from lead toxicity and its long-term effects is to avoid it altogether. However, this is of course not always within the control of the individual and a second best bet is to have the lead removed via chelation as a protective measure against its undoubted toxicity which can contribute towards the evolution of cancer.

Australian research scientist John Sterling, who has worked at the famous Issels clinic in Germany, mentions in a personal communication that Issels had noted a marked protective effect against cancer after use of EDTA chelation.

Animal studies (using mice) have shown that intravenous EDTA plays a preventive role against cancer, largely, it is thought, through removal of metallic ions which seem to be essential for tumour growth.

Walker and Gordon believe that the prevention offered to the citizens of Zurich was partly as a result of removal of metal ions and of lead (which can chronically depress immune function) and also due to the improvement in circulation which chelation produced. Tumours flourish in areas of poor oxygenation and the increase in the levels of this which chelation allows would, they believe, be sufficient to retard cancer development.

Halstead (1979) points to the significant increase in metal ions found as tissues age and the increased likelihood of cancer developing. There is also a proven link between high levels of certain metals in topsoil and cancer in the same regions. Interestingly, he confirms that most forms of chemotherapy involve drugs which have chelating effects either directly or as a result of breakdown of their constituents. He quotes experimental studies which show that in some forms of cancer such as Ehrlich's ascites tumour the use of EDTA was significantly able to strip the tumour cells of their heavy protective coat, allowing other mechanisms (such as protein digesting enzymes) to destroy the tumours.

At the very least EDTA chelation can be seen to offer a useful line of investigation in cancer prevention, and possibly treatment, in some forms of this disease.

Benefits for some mental problems

Dr Wayne Perry (1988) comments on one of the beneficial 'side-effects' of EDTA therapy when he states: 'Those who have used EDTA have been impressed by the dramatic effects that can occur in some patients, and this action might be explained by its powerful anti-depressant effect, shown in a double blind trial over and above any placebo action.' (See Kay *et al* 1984.) In discussing the objective evidence of general improvement amongst patients having EDTA he includes 'general alertness, concentration and memory' as common.

Clearly, if circulation to the brain is enhanced the function of that organ should improve. Equally important to mental function would be the removal of heavy metals, the toxicity of which are common causes of a wide range of problems affecting the brain and nervous system. It should therefore not be surprising that EDTA often leads to improved memory and reduced tendency to depression and other apparently 'psychological' symptoms.

The research team of McDonagh, Rudolph and Cheraskin have looked at just this aspect of EDTA chelation therapy's effect – the psychotherapeutic benefits. (McDonagh, Rudolph and Cheraskin, 1984, 1985a, 1985b) They used a standard medical questionnaire (Cornell Medical Index – see Brodman *et al* 1949) at the first consultation to allow 139 routine private-practice patients, 83 of whom were male, to answer questions from which 'depression', 'tension' and 'anger' tendencies could be discovered. These same patients completed the same questionnaire at the end of a series of EDTA infusions (plus multimineral/vitamin support supplementation) over a two-month period. There was a 40 per cent reduction in depression indications amongst those patients who showed a tendency towards depression in their first questionnaire. There was a 50 per cent reduction in 'tension' symptoms and a 46 per cent reduction in 'anger' indications at the end of the treatment period.

The researchers speculate that the improvement was due to overall improvement in cellular nutrition as a result of the enhanced circulation due to this form of treatment. They note that the improvements in emotional status, observed in this study, were superior in degree to any physical improvements noted in their many previous studies.

General symptoms and fatigue reduced after EDTA therapy

Using the same approach these researchers had over 100 patients complete the whole Cornell Medical Index (CMI) questionnaire before and after a chelation series which averaged 26 infusions over a two-month period. The CMI questionnaire is designed to collect a great deal of information in a short space of time. Anyone with more than 25 positive answers out of the 195 questions is considered to be suffering from a significant degree of current ill-health.

Before treatment, the average number of positive answers amongst these patients was 31.7, indicating an overall poor level of health. Some patients had as many as 95 'Yes' answers, with the lowest score being 3; more than half of the patients had over 25 positive answers. When the CMI questionnaire was answered again after the therapy series there was a drop of 46 per cent in those with more than 25 positive answers and the overall number of symptoms reported dropped by 15 per cent.

The CMI is divided into different sections and when these were analysed for before-and-after changes, the pattern that emerged was as follows:

> Musculoskeletal symptoms declined by 25 per cent; neurological symptoms by 19 per cent; cardiovascular by 19 per cent; skin conditions by 18 per cent; respiratory by 17 per cent; genital by 13 per cent; gastro-intestinal by 11 per cent and urinary by 11 per cent.

Specific attention was paid to fatigue in these patients, as this general symptom is amongst the commonest and most worrying for many people in poor health. Seven questions in the CMI relate specifically to the degree of fatigue/tiredness felt. The percentage of those answering this section who had no fatigue symptoms rose from 31 per cent to 56 per cent over the course of the treatment series, and of those originally reporting fatigue as a symptom, fully 39 per cent showed an appreciable improvement. Since most researchers and therapists involved in chelation therapy report that the greatest beneficial effect is not felt until up to 90 days after the cessation of therapy, these results may well indicate only the beginning of the benefits ultimately achieved.

Considering the fact that over half those involved were by any definition in very poor health, the improvements were remarkable, and the very general nature of their spread supports the contention of these researchers that they were due to generalized nutritional enhancement due to circulatory improvements resulting from EDTA therapy.

Chapter 6

The chelation protocol

Before chelation infusion therapy is started a detailed study should be made of the patient to ensure that this is an appropriate approach to the problem(s) of the individual.

A full medical case history and examination is the first prerequisite, including a comprehensive personal and family history detailing all aspects of previous health problems and current status. Questions relating to diet, habits, emotional status, exercise, stress levels and a detailed listing of symptoms is part of this. A full physical examination is also required, most notably of all aspects of the circulatory and respiratory systems.

An electrocardiogram and chest X-ray might be required as well as a number of blood tests. Exercise tolerance tests may be used to see just how the functioning of the heart, lungs and circulation responds to activity. A commonly used procedure, before chelation therapy is started, and of major importance in establishing a 'before' picture of circulatory efficiency, is the use of what is known as bi-directional Doppler (sound wave) examination.

Doppler test

This is a painless, non-invasive use of sound waves (ultrasonic) which is used to investigate six major arterial sites which relate to circulation to the brain, as well as eight sites which relate to circulation to the legs. The Doppler equipment gives readings which tell the doctor running the tests three important pieces of information at each site:

1   It shows whether there is any turbulence which could relate to breakaway deposits of plaque, etc., which could be involved in production of a stroke.

2   It checks for any signs of capillary hardening in the brain, often associated with memory loss and age-related brain changes.
3   The major arteries are assessed for obstructions to normal flow of blood which could relate to over-burdened heart function or deficient circulation to the legs.

This sound-wave testing takes about an hour and all findings are recorded on charts so that later tests can be compared. This is also an excellent way for the patient to appreciate visually the degree of current circulatory difficulty.

Thermography

Use of thermographically (heat) sensitive film allows areas of the body which are not receiving their full circulatory servicing to be photographed as a record which can be compared with the same region after treatment.

Blood tests

Among other tests, an initial one is performed (not for people with diabetes) after overnight fasting (14 hours without food). This test is usually done around mid-morning, the last food (or coffee or sugar) having been consumed around 9 pm the previous night. The fasting blood test gives an accurate idea of cholesterol levels as well as other key markers. Periodic monitoring of blood levels of cholesterol and other elements (giving evidence of levels of blood fats, carbohydrates, whether or not there is anaemia, infection, immune system problems, liver or kidney dysfunction, etc.) is made during the chelation treatment which can last for some months, with two or three infusions per week.

Depending upon the condition of the patient a blood sample may be required before each treatment, or periodically.

Urine test

A 24-hour sample is required for assessment of normal urinary output of creatinine, a key guide as to kidney status. A periodic assessment is made of the creatinine levels of the urine as the series of chelation treatments progress, but this does not require collection of 24-hour samples. As with blood testing, the frequency of urine testing during a series of chelation infusions will vary, depending on the nature of the problem being treated and the health of the patient.

If there is any evidence that the kidneys could not be expected to deal efficiently with the elimination of EDTA during infusion, then the treatment series would be delayed or stopped until this factor had been dealt with appropriately. As we will see in a description of important research by Doctors McDonagh, Rudolph and Cheraskin later in this chapter, kidney dysfunction is often capable of being normalized by EDTA chelation therapy.

Diet and other tests

A computerized dietary analysis (based on the filling in of lengthy questionnaires) of what the patient eats is often required so that comprehensive dietary and supplementation advice can be given to the person being chelated, to complement the treatment.

In addition, saliva, sweat and faeces may need to be tested for a variety of reasons, including assessment of what the patient's current metabolic and nutrient status is, how well foods are being digested and absorbed, etc. Whether such tests are needed will depend upon the individual problems being dealt with.

Hair analysis

This non-invasive and inexpensive method is also sometimes used to provide an accurate indication of heavy metal toxicity as well as to give some idea of the current mineral status of the body. The findings from this and the other tests allow the doctor in charge to decide just what balance of minerals should be added to the basic EDTA infusion solution in order to obtain the best results.

EDTA treatment

Once it has been established that there is a problem which could benefit from EDTA infusion, a series of treatments are scheduled, either two or three times per week. Most chelation centres treat patients in a group setting.

A large room with appropriate seating (usually comfortable recliners) is all that is needed (not unlike a hairdressing or beauty salon). There are several advantages to this approach:

1   The mutual support of people having the same procedure is reassuring and encouraging. There will almost always be someone present who has had a number of infusions and who can give a personal account of what to expect.
2   The costs can be reduced, since fewer supervisory staff are required if patients are grouped together in this way.
3   During the 3½ hours of the infusion the patient can read, doze, chat, watch TV, listen to a pep talk on diet or exercise from a clinician (this is a truly 'captive audience').

The infusion itself involves the insertion into a vein (usually in the hand or forearm, but sometimes the lower leg) of a needle which is attached to the container (hung on an adjustable stand), from which is drip-fed around half a litre of fluid over the 3½ hours' duration of each treatment. This liquid usually contains 2 to 3 grams of EDTA and whatever additional minerals the doctor has decided will best help achieve a balanced blood content.

EDTA mixture
Among the other substances often placed in solution with the EDTA are a complex of B vitamins, vitamin C, magnesium (extremely useful for cardiovascular health) and heparin (an anti-coagulant, enough of which is sometimes used just to prevent any clotting at the injection site). Cranton suggests (Cranton and Frackelton, 1982) that since magnesium is a natural calcium antagonist and also the ion least likely to be removed by EDTA (see Chapter 4), and that it is relatively deficient in many people with cardiovascular and circulatory problems, it should be supplied with the chelation process. He suggests that the best way to do this is to use magnesium-EDTA, which would provide an efficient delivery system and thereby increase magnesium stores in the body.

When the infusion is being performed, the arm is kept stable as a rule by being taped to a padded board which rests on a cushion for comfort. It is usually quite possible (although it is not encouraged) for the patient to move around freely during treatment (to visit the toilet, for example) as long as the mobile infusion is wheeled alongside.

The rate at which the EDTA solution is dripped into the bloodstream can be varied but usually it is at a rate of one drop per second.

As a general rule, two, but sometimes three, treatments are given each week, and a total of anything from 20 (for relatively mild problems) to 30 infusions in all comprise one complete series.

On a number of occasions (sometimes at each visit) blood and urine testing (as well as other tests) may be carried out to ensure that kidney and other functions are operating sufficiently well to cope with the EDTA detoxification. This is obviously more important in elderly patients or anyone with compromised kidney function. In some instances where a great deal of circulatory pathology exists, follow-up series of chelation infusions might be encouraged, with many people showing benefits after up to 100 infusions.

The EDTA is eliminated from the body, 95 per cent via the kidneys and 5 per cent via the bile, along with the toxic metals and free ionic calcium which it has locked on to in its transit through the circulatory system.

In hospital settings, EDTA infusions have in the past been given daily for up to five days, followed by a two-day rest period for the kidneys. This protocol is now discouraged by the American medical group with the most experience of chelation, the American Academy of Medical Preventics.

Toxicity and cautions

General toxicity

Walker and Gordon (1982) inform us that EDTA is far safer than aspirin, digoxin, tetracyclin, ethyl alcohol or the nicotine from two cigarettes, in equivalent therapeutic doses. EDTA is used in thousands of food products (it is in most canned foods) and its toxicity is known to be extremely low.

In assessing the relative toxicity of a substance a therapeutic index is established. Firstly, the amount of the substance which would prove lethal to half the animals in an experimental setting is discovered by the gruesome process of increasing their intake until half of them die. This is the LD-50 measurement (LD for lethal dose). When this amount is divided by the amount required for a therapeutic effect we end with a number which is the therapeutic index.

The LD-50 of EDTA is 2000 milligrams per kilo of body weight, whether taken orally or intravenously. In comparison aspirin has a toxicity equal to 558 milligrams per kilo of body weight. So in general there is no need for concern as to general toxicity with EDTA usage, whether by mouth (see Chapter 9) or directly into the blood.

Kidney toxicity
In the early 1950s several deaths occurred from nephrotoxicity after EDTA treatment. At that time the dosage used was around 10 grams per infusion, whereas the recommended dose nowadays is 3 grams.

Halstead (1979) states:

> The problem in EDTA nephrotoxicity is based upon two fundamental principles of toxicology: dosage and route of administration. Dosage is concerned with both the amount administered and the rate of administration, or the time period in which the EDTA is given.

It appears that toxicity for the kidneys may relate directly to too large a dose infused at too fast a rate. In general, if no more than 3 grams is infused in any 24-hour period (diluted with 500 ml sterile Lactated Ringer's solution or — except in the case of diabetes — 5 per cent dextrose solution), with a 24-hour rest period between chelation infusions (2-3 per week) and if the infusion of these 3 grams (less than 50 milligrams per kilo of body weight) is timed to take around three hours, little if any danger exists of producing toxicity for the kidneys.

Indeed, research has shown that in general chelation therapy improves kidney function, particularly if any impairment to these vital organs relates to circulatory problems.

Improved kidney function after EDTA
McDonagh, Rudolph and Cheraskin (1982d) have investigated the alleged toxicity of EDTA in relation to kidney function and their results are worth some consideration.

They examined the results of treating 383 people with a variety of chronic degenerative disorders (primarily occlusive arterial disease) with EDTA chelation therapy (plus supportive multivitamin/mineral supplementation) for 50 days.

The measurement of the levels of creatinine in the blood is commonly used in medicine as a guide to kidney efficiency.

Creatinine is the end breakdown product of muscle activity which is cleared from the body by filtration through the normal kidney. The levels found in the bloodstream are known to correlate well with the rate and efficiency of clearance, giving a simple way of judging kidney function. The researchers made specific measurements of the levels of creatinine in the blood of these patients at the first visit (fasting levels) and then gave 10 infusions of 3 grams of EDTA in a solution of 1000 cc normal saline with an interval of five days between each infusion (supplementation was also given). After this the serum creatinine was again assessed.

They found that a very interesting balancing effect could be seen when the overall picture was revealed, very similar to that noted when cholesterol ratios were examined (see Chapter 4). Those people who initially had low levels of serum creatinine showed a very slight increase; those in the mid-range (normal?) showed no change and those above the mid-range of normal and actually with a creatinine excess (therefore indicating poor clearance by the kidneys) showed a drop towards normal.

Overall the total measurement showed an average decline in serum levels (indicating improved kidney function), but far more significant, according to the judgement of the researchers, is the homoeostatic effect in which – whether high or low to start with – a tendency towards the mid-range (between 0.5 and 1.7 milligrams/decilitre) is observed.

It seems that EDTA therapy may actually improve kidney function *if it is applied slowly with normal dosages.*

One exception

These researchers make note of one exceptional case amongst nearly 400 patients tested in this way, and the progression of events is worth noting as an example which highlights both the initial concerns which some patients might produce and the long-term benefits of chelation therapy.

This was an 86-year-old female in whom the initial measurement of creatinine was 1.9 mg/dl, which is regarded as abnormally high and therefore indicative of poor kidney function. After starting chelation every five days, a rise was seen in the creatinine levels by day 25 (fifth infusion) to a very unhealthy 3.5 mg/dl. As treatment progressed, it dropped to 2.8 mg/dl by day 60 and had dropped to 1.8 mg/dl by day 100, some time after the course of chelation therapy had finished.

As the researchers point out: 'this emphasizes the need to follow renal function during EDTA therapy', and, one might add, for a while after, as the benefits frequently are not fully manifest before about three months after treatment is over.

Special considerations: age, heavy metals or parathyroid deficiency

If the patient is very elderly, or has low parathyroid activity or is suffering from heavy metal toxicity which is damaging kidney tubules, treatment should be modified to use less EDTA less frequently (once weekly perhaps). Heavy metals damage the kidneys and too rapid infusion can overload them. Heavy metals most likely to produce kidney damage during infusion therapy (if this is done too rapidly, that is) are lead, aluminium, cadmium, mercury, nickel, copper and arsenic.

Renal function tests should always be performed before chelation therapy is started in which serum nitrogen (BUN) and serum creatinine is examined. In any case of significant renal impairment, lower dosage EDTA infusions should be used with extreme caution with suitable periods of rest between.

Too much calcium removed

If, through inexperience or error, there is too rapid an infusion (or too much EDTA used), levels of calcium in the blood can drop rapidly, resulting in cramps, tetany, convulsions, etc. An injection of calcium gluconate will swiftly control such abnormal reactions. This hypocalcaemia reaction is almost unheard of where the guidelines given above are followed as to dosage, speed of infusion and spread of treatments.

Inflammation of a vein

If an infusion into a vein is performed too rapidly, inflammation may occur (thrombophlebitis). This is unlikely in the extreme if guidelines as described above are followed concerning dilution of EDTA with Ringer's solution or dextrose solution and slow infusion.

Should the needle carrying the infusion slip, a local soft tissue irritation may develop. This may best be treated with use of alternate hot and cold packs. Supplementation with anti-oxidant nutrients such as vitamins C and E (make sure of a good source) and the mineral selenium should protect against such an incident.

Care regarding insulin shock and hypoglycaemia

During EDTA infusion it is possible for blood glucose to drop, leading to insulin shock. This is more likely amongst diabetics in whom no dextrose solution should be used. Patients having EDTA infusions are advised to have a snack before or during the three hours plus treatment period. Walker and Gordon (1982) recommend the following strategy:

> You should eat something before the three to four hour infusions, but not high-calcium-containing foods such as dairy products. Rather, eat adequate unrefined complex carbohydrates and avoid most sugars, including overripe bananas.

During an infusion they recommend eating fruit.

In diabetic individuals, using zinc-bound insulin involves a risk of too rapid a release of insulin, leading to hypoglycaemia and shock. A rapid introduction of sugar is needed in such an instance and a change in the form of insulin used before further EDTA infusions are tried. Most people with known diabetes find that with chelation therapy their requirement for insulin declines.

Congestive heart failure

If the heart is already unable to cope adequately with movement of fluids, and there is evidence of congestive heart failure (extreme shortness of breath, swollen ankles) and/or if digitalis-like medication is being taken, extreme care is needed over chelation infusions, since EDTA prevents digitalis working adequately. Sodium EDTA would appear to be undesirable in such people as it could increase the fluid retention tendency. However, Halstead is adamant that:

> Na_2 EDTA does not appear to have any significant deleterious effects in congestive heart patients since the sodium (Na_2) is apparently excreted intact with the metal chelate. However, the use of 5 per cent dextrose and water is recommended in such cases.

Short-term side-effects

A number of variable side-effects have been observed with use of intravenous EDTA infusion, including the following:

● *Headaches* – which often relate to the same phenomenon

discussed above, of low blood sugar. Eating before treatment, or during it, will usually prevent this possibility. It is reported that a common recommendation which prevents 'EDTA-headaches' is that a banana, not overripe, be eaten during the first hour of infusion.

- *Diarrhoea* – this unusual side-effect should be treated with rest and a bland diet with plenty of liquids for a day or so.
- *Urinary frequency* is common as kidney efficiency improves and a weight loss (from fluid excretion) of 3-5 pounds (1.3-2.2 kg) is common after an infusion if fluid retention was previously evident.
- *Local skin irritation* may result and is usually associated with a reduction in zinc and vitamin B6 (pyridoxine). For this reason supplementation of these nutrients is usually suggested during chelation therapy.
- *Nausea or stomach upset* may also be related to vitamin B6 deficiency in the less than one patient in 100 receiving chelation therapy who feels this side-effect. It is best treated by B6 supplementation, although short-term relief (up to eight hours) from nausea can be achieved by applying thumb pressure to a point two thumb-widths above the wrist crease on either forearm (acupuncture point P6) for a minute or so whenever the symptom is felt.
- *Feeling faint* may relate to a drop in blood pressure. It is common for those who start treatment with high blood pressure to see a return to more normal levels. If it were normal to start with, it could drop slightly as well as leading to feelings of faintness on standing after sitting or lying. Treatment is to rest for an hour or so when this happens, ideally with the feet slightly higher than the head. The amino acid tyrosine can safely be supplemented to help restore normal pressure levels if this symptom persists.
- *Fever* may develop in a very few people during the day after chelation therapy sessions (approximately one in 5000). Whoever is in charge of the treatment should be told, although the condition normally resolves on its own.
- *Extreme fatigue* may be felt in some people and this is usually the result of a general nutrient deficiency in minerals such as magnesium, zinc or potassium. Taking a potassium-rich supplement and/or the regular eating of potassium-rich foods is suggested before and during chelation (grapes, bananas, peaches, potato skins), as this

mineral may be removed by the process itself.

- *Pains in the joints* are more likely where infusions are frequent (three weekly). An immediate reduction to once weekly is suggested, and also possibly a reduction in dosage of EDTA being used, if strong flu-like aches develop. The symptoms should pass fairly soon if these strategies are adopted.
- *Cramps* in the legs are not uncommon (one patient in 20), usually at night. The supplementation of magnesium (either by mouth or in the EDTA infusions) will usually prevent this happening. If it is added to the infusion this could be in the form of magnesium chloride or magnesium sulphate. Such additions also reduce the chance of local skin irritation at the site of the infusion.

Other minor side-effects have been reported in the many millions of chelation infusions already given, but all seem to vanish when the therapy is reduced or stopped. As Bruce Halstead states: 'The number of significant untoward reactions is probably less than in any other major therapeutic modality.'

Chapter 7

Case histories
(by Simon Martin)

Heart disease

Harvard University asked more than 22,000 doctors, all at least 40 years old, to take aspirin every day for four years. By then, 104 had heart attacks; five were fatal. In contrast, of those who took an inactive dummy pill, 189 had heart attacks and 18 died.

Doctors have got excited about these results because, while 500 people a day die of heart disease in the UK, the drugs used to prevent this happening have some unwanted effects and have not been proved to be totally effective. Aspirin, on the other hand, is universally regarded as safe, cheap and convenient.

But even as the Americans stampeded to their medicine cabinets (helped by a massive publicity campaign mounted by aspirin manufacturers), warnings were sounded by British experts. Sir Richard Doll points out that if aspirin helps people who have already had heart attacks, then it does so at the expense of causing more strokes. The benefits to healthy people are even less obvious.

This sounds familiar. International authorities have recommended that anyone with higher than average levels of cholesterol circulating in the blood should start corrective treatment with drugs. Yet the Helsinki Heart Study (on 19,000 men aged 40-55), the World Health Organization study (on 10,000 men), and the Lipid Research Clinics Coronary Primary Prevention trial (3,800 'at risk' men), have all shown that any reduction in the number of expected deaths from heart disease is balanced by an increase in deaths from other causes.

The implication is that these may be caused by the 'preventive' drugs themselves; an idea supported by the many non-fatal effects reported in the drug users. These include more gastro-intestinal complications (and surgery to put them right), more gallstones and more cataracts.

Because of this predilection to use drugs as preventive medicine, many people are becoming wary of health screening. Having regular check-ups, particularly if they involve an enthusiastic, interventionist doctor who monitors blood pressure and goes in for cardiograms and stress tests, may actually be dangerous to health.

Aspirin, too, is not the innocuous substance it is made out to be. Children's aspirin was withdrawn from over-the-counter sale after many years of assumed safe use. It causes gastro-intestinal bleeding and pain. Drugs, it seems, are a very poor form of preventive medicine.

The irony is that we have all the information we need to stop heart disease without drugs. Evidence is that these alternatives are not only safe and effective ways of staying alive, but that they can actually reverse the process of conditions like atherosclerosis, even at the emergency stage when a man is scheduled for bypass surgery.

That was the experience of Richard B, a 42-year-old businessman and amateur athletics coach, who remembers running a fast track 200 metres in the middle of the pack, floating easily across the finish line – and waking up in intensive care.

He knew about diet and exercise and it hadn't saved him from a heart attack. It turned out that he was genetically unable to produce a cholesterol-controlling enzyme. Unable to walk after his spectacular collapse, he was whisked to the front of the waiting list and booked in for double bypass surgery. The operation was due to take place the day after his wedding.

He was too doubtful to go in for it. Bypass surgery is not a permanent solution and is frequently ineffective. A 1,000-man study by the American Veterans Administration found that bypass surgery was of no benefit for anyone but those with the rare left-main artery disease. Bypassing clogged arteries is one thing; but what about the ones that are left? These too will become clogged, and more surgery will be needed, until the unfortunate patient runs out of replacement tissue. It makes much more sense to do something about root causes.

Richard opted instead for chelation. This treatment, combined with a low-fat, high-fibre, low-sugar diet, and supplements of vitamins and minerals, enabled Richard to report to his disbelieving consultant three months later that he was back in athletics training and did not need any operation.

The consultant wanted to conduct an angiogram, in which a dye is injected into the arteries and examined under X-rays. Richard refused, because during a previous angiogram his heart had stopped while he was on the table.

There was no real need. Here was a man who couldn't walk because of the pains in his chest, now back to an hour's running – not jogging – a day, plus circuit training, and all without drugs.

Besides, American scientists had already established a precedent, with a paper published in 1977 in the Annals of Internal Medicine. Their patients, average age 48, all had angiograms to diagnose extensive blockage due to atherosclerosis. After 13 months on a low-fat diet they were angiogrammed again: in nearly half, the existing deposits of arterial plaque had begun to disappear. With the known benefits of chelation, and the technology to check on how the arteries are functioning without invasive measures, Richard felt confident to refuse more surgery.

His case is typical of those gathered in the files of chelation centres throughout the world. And from those supplied by the Chelation Centre, London, for this book, it is clear that even though their cases are supervised by a consultant physician and endocrinologist and have full test data available, many doctors and surgeons find it very difficult to believe that their patients have been able to recover so well.

One professor of cardiology at a leading American university school of medicine confirmed the excellent physical status of a patient who had used chelation therapy, but felt moved to add a handwritten postscript: 'As you know I really don't believe chelation is effective!'

All good closing-of-the-ranks stuff. Unfortunately, this dubious sort of behaviour is resulting in a safe and effective treatment being denied patients – not on the basis of serious scientific analysis, but as a result of sniggering humour.

The patient who made this correspondence available was a man aged over 60 who had received a triple bypass operation at this same American university. Six weeks later he began to experience severe recurrent angina. At first he responded to calcium channel blocking drugs, but after a few more months his angina got so bad that he was unable to walk.

On his own initiative, and still suffering despite the best that high-tech medicine could offer, he began chelation therapy. He had 20 treatments in all. Eight months after his first chelation session he reported back to the university: he was totally without symptoms. Not only was he able to walk, but was walking up hills and was working a full day. No shortness of breath, no side-effects from the chelation.

His physical examination proved his blood pressure to be 150/90. His pulse was 77. His chest was clear. His heart not enlarged, and with a murmur and a '4th heart sound'. He had stopped all his drugs two weeks before the examination, because he was feeling and functioning so well. 'As you know I really don't believe chelation is effective!' The only comment.

If this was an isolated case of benefit, where calcium blockers and operations and/or surgical operations had brought no relief, then perhaps it would be understandable. But the evidence has been accumulating for years; and patients who have tried, or who want to try, chelation must by now be very familiar to American heart surgeons.

The attitude in Britain is little better, although perhaps slightly less aggressively and blindly 'anti'. In fact, a patient who wrote to the British Heart Foundation, the heart research charity, for their opinion on chelation was told, quite reasonably, that there were two sides to the argument and there was no reason at all why he should not explore the matter for himself.

But the BHF also passed on another example of deeply entrenched dogma. They told him:

> You may or may not be aware that chelation therapy has been around for some 30 years and opinions regarding its value vary enormously . . . One of our professors who is an expert on atheromatous coronary artery disease and has done a lot of research on it recently summed up the situation by saying that the evidence of benefit is almost non-existent and the experimental basis for supposed advantage is very weak. The general consensus of opinion seems to be that there is no advantage over calcium antagonists such as Adalat.

The BHF has made no secret of the fact that it has funded a lot of research into this group of drugs over the years.

Mr SC, another 60-year-old, was also a victim of this dogma when, following angioplasty – surgery to repair the blood vessels in his chest – in the heart unit of the prestigious Stanford

University School of Medicine in California, he experienced considerable pain from 'residual' angina. This side-effect of surgery had been predicted, but not the degree.

He was placed on calcium blockers, a high dose of six 10 mg tablets three times a day. Even so, the angina did not stop. After only two chelation infusions, the angina disappeared.

This story had a happy ending. Mr SC's regular doctor (he does not live in America) is a cardiac surgeon. And when Mr SC returned home after chelation, this doctor was so impressed he proposed to use angioplasty and chelation as complementary treatments in future. The patient reports this surgeon's more open-minded view of the process:

> His opinion is that EDTA removes only a microscopic layer of plaque (as well as smoothing the artery wall due to healing of the cells that line the arteries). He feels, however, that the removal of even a microscopic layer of plaque in arterioles supplying blood to artery muscles could improve blood flow to the artery muscles substantially and would likely prevent artery spasm, thereby preventing much angina pain in an extraordinarily short space of time.

What can chelation achieve in a patient with heart problems? Let's follow the history of one man in more detail. (As with all case histories, I am grateful to the late James Kavanagh of the Chelation Centre of London and Pagham, West Sussex, for providing full data. Names of patients have been changed and, unless their specific permission was given, have only been identified to me by initials.)

The case we'll follow is of a 62-year-old man whose chief complaint was angina. This had come on after surgery to his prostate and was so severe that it used to wake him up, on average, three times a night. Luckily for us, this gentleman is scientifically trained and kept precise notes of his progress before, during and after the chelation programme.

In addition, we have access to the reports of two doctors he consulted for examinations during 1982, when his severe angina began after his prostate operation, and a full proposal for treatment from a specialist in an American coronary unit. This surgeon had seen the previous medical records and from them suspected 'significant' disease of our man's coronary arteries. Subject to a full physical examination in the United States, the proposal moved on to plans for surgery and warned of a possible cost of up to $20,000, a sum of money which puts into perspective the comparatively modest cost of chelation.

An opinion from the chief of this American unit was that our patient – let's call him George – would need an angiogram and probable angioplasty, with possible bypass surgery. George was told to proceed 'immediately' with this schedule, and certainly not to leave it longer than two months. His angina by then had become unstable.

George did not have the bypass. His angina 'virtually ceased' after his first chelation infusion. But we're getting ahead of ourselves.

George's problems really started in 1972. A specialist professional in a demanding job, he had an episode of dizziness and his doctor found his blood pressure had got way too high. To control it he was first given Reserpine, a drug isolated from the Rauwolfia plant, whose constituents are a traditional sedative. Reserpine pulls out of the tissues, nerve endings and the brain, circulating chemicals that act on blood vessels to raise blood pressure.

One of Reserpine's side-effects is that it can affect mood, and George's blood pressure medication was changed several times over the years until he had finally settled on two Catapres tablets a day. Catapres contains clonidine, a chemical which works on the central nervous system. It reduces blood pressure, slows the heart and is a mild sedative. It does nothing to treat the root causes of high blood pressure, but effectively does away with the symptoms – the body's warning signals that something is wrong and needs attention.

Towards the end of the 1970s, George was bothered by a fluctuation in his heartbeat and occasional chest pains. That was addressed with a prescription for two tablets of Trasicor a day. Trasicor is based on oxyprenolol, which is one of the class of drugs known as beta-blockers. These chemicals are firm favourites of some professional musicians, who find public performances so nerve-racking that they are unable to play, and even some sports people. The beta-blockers work by blocking nerve endings called beta-receptors. These are the receptors that pick up nerve stimulus to the heart – which can be sent down the line due to emotional stress, fear, aggression, tension and so on. The nerve signals, if received, would normally cause the heart to increase its work rate – so it beats faster.

Beta-blockers are also used to treat angina, as if there are any deficiencies in the arteries supplying blood to the heart, when the nerve signals speed up the heart, the increased flow of blood against the resistance of a restricted artery can cause severe pain.

George didn't experience full angina, though, until a few years later. In 1982 he had microsurgery on an enlarged prostate gland. Despite the drugs he was using, immediately after the operation he developed severe angina and was put on oxygen for three days. In an effort to control the angina, he was given two more drugs to take in addition to the two he was already taking. These were Nitrobid (four a day), a drug which relaxes the walls of blood vessels, reducing the amount of blood flowing to and from the heart; and Dyazide, later changed to three capsules of Adalat a day.

Adalat is one of a class of drugs known as 'calcium antagonists', an interesting choice knowing what we know about chelation's effects on calcium. Adalat works by slowing the entry of calcium (carried in the blood) into the heart and blood vessels. The idea is to prevent the flow of blood from 'silting up'; again, they do nothing to address the underlying problem.

By the time George's angina became worrying – despite all these drugs – it was the end of 1985. By then he reported his symptoms as:

- Blood pressure of 180 or 170/100 without medication, controlled at about 145 or 150/95 with medication.
- Onset of angina after four hours of working in the office, needing Nitrobid to control it.
- Regular waking at night: three times, sometimes four times a night, needing more Nitrobid and sleeping pills to allow sleep.
- 'Permanent feeling of lack of air (oxygen), requiring rooms to have low temperatures and windows open even on coldest nights. Inability to remain by a fireside or to sit in stuffy rooms, trains, shops, etc. I could not remain in a heated shop for more than a few minutes.'
- Ability to walk only about one and a half miles (2.4 km) at steady pace, and not up hills or steps. Shortness of breath.
- Heavy chest pressure at end of day's work.
- 'General malaise and disinterest in life, with condition and sleeplessness interacting to provide general deterioration in health.'

Christmas with the family was not pleasant. 'Life was difficult for my family due to my inability to stay in a room at a comfortable temperature,' said George.

At that point, faced with a recommendation for a $20,000 bypass operation with no guarantee of improvement afterwards, an old friend in Nairobi, Kenya, suggested that George investigate chelation, since doctors in Nairobi had successfully treated numbers of people with similar conditions.

Treatment began on 15 January, 1986 after series of tests and I continued with my previous dosage of Catapres, Trasicor, Nitrobid and Adalat.

After first chelation infusion, angina virtually ceased with no 'reminding' pains to call for the next medication due. Felt much brighter and began to make plans for remainder of year. Began to sleep properly, with maximum of one waking per night, but still with windows open, however cold.

After second treatment on the 17th, found I could lie in bed on left side for 20 minutes before turning to right. Previously this was possible for only a few minutes. I had a feeling of some movement at left side of heart on Monday, 20th and Tuesday, 21st. Had severe *heartburn* in night due to acidity as a result of taking too many "make-up" yellow chelation supplement pills. This caused racing of heart and was assuaged by taking Milk of Magnesia antacid pills. Quite frightening at the time.

On Monday morning, 10th February, after taking one Nitrocontin tablet with early morning tea, had a pain of some sort across top of heart. Before chelation, I usually had 'relaxation' pain in this place after taking nitroglycerin. Only one single, non-sharp, pain was felt. During the morning I noticed specks of white material up to $\frac{1}{16}$ inch (1.5mm) or more across with white vapour trails swirling slowly in my urine.

Throughout the first eight infusions, I gradually began to feel better, with much improved attitude to life. I began to breathe easily without the feeling that there was chewing gum stuck around my heart. I found I could sleep in a heated room with minimum ventilation, shovel snow slowly and do jobs around the house with enthusiasm again. Also, at various times during chelation, I had a 'feeling' at weekends that something around my heart was moving – not a pain, but a 'feeling', first on top and left side, then underneath and then at back of heart, etc.

I had had arterial pains in my right calf and ankle swelling in my left ankle (especially after flying) before chelation. This was described as venous thrombosis by Dr T. I felt some slight pain in the right calf artery and in the veins of my right leg during the second week of chelation. Thereafter the pains, both right arterial and varicose, ceased.

After eight infusions I felt altogether better. I reduced my Nitrocontin tablets (Nitrobid not available in UK) from four to three per day on 31st January, also Adalat capsules from three to two per day. On 7th February, I reduced my two Catapres tablets per day to one. I expected to reduce my Nitrocontin further, but Dr P required me to continue with this reduced dose until the end of treatment.

I can now write for ten hours, with considerable concentration and without onset of angina. I think I see colours more brightly. No change was noticeable to general vision or hearing, but a change of glasses did improve vision.

From eighth infusion onwards to the twentieth my ability to walk quite fast for long distances became much improved, including walking non-stop up a fairly steep long hill near my house. I have continued to feel 'movements' at weekends in various parts of my body, including right side of head and a return to top side, underneath and back of heart. I now sleep through the night regularly with normal minimum of room ventilation. I sometimes need a sleeping pill the night after an infusion.

I cleared a 5 inch (12.5cm) depth of snow from our house drive and footpaths (quite extensive) at beginning of March.

After the twelfth infusion my BP was down to 130/80 despite reduction of BP-reducing pills. I reduced my Nitroglycerin to 1½ (2.5 mg) tablets per day.

After the twentieth infusion, I had very definite movement activity all around my heart on the Saturday night and this woke me from sleep. It subsided without medication and I felt similar movements in the centre of my right calf. I wondered whether this was debris or plaque being moved. The faint feeling or slight pain in right calf remained. On Sunday, I slept well again.

I feel the treatment has done all that I could have possibly hoped for and after a few months' rest I intend to have more chelation infusions.

I have lost weight (about 8lb/3.6kg) but am still 5 or 6lb (2.5kg) overweight. At or around the twelfth-fifteenth infusion, I developed excess fluid around my heart and could feel slight bubbling beneath my heart at night. This was confirmed by X-ray and Dr P advised cutting fluids while on chelation. This I did and I believe the fluid had gradually dissipated by the end of the treatment.

I informed Dr P of the slight 'pain' in my right calf. This was possibly brought about by my climbing 190 steps non-stop one day.

Six weeks have gone by since my treatment ceased on 21 March, and the pain in my right calf and a slight pain at the back of my right knee have now virtually disappeared and I do not feel them even on morning waking (as I did before chelation).

A few months after completing his chelation programme, George reported: 'I am feeling fine, though working a nine-hour day. I think in future it would be better to cease the work stress and I have this in mind a year from now!'

'Smoker's legs' and claudication

'Probably the most seriously ill person whom we have treated,' is how Chelation Centre's James Kavanagh described the lady whose case history we next look at.

'Smoker's legs' is the slang description for her condition. We'll refer to her as Eileen (not her real name). She was 64 years old when she arrived for treatment, barely able to walk even with a stick.

About 13 years before she had needed a heart operation to fix up her aorta, the huge artery growing out of the heart from which a complete system of arteries develops. It had become blocked, and the operation was described as 'aorto-iliac reconstruction', in which the 'bifurcation was cleared out completely and was widened with a heart-shaped patch'.

Unfortunately for Eileen, her condition had continued to deteriorate despite this excellent – and literal – unblocking and patching-up job. She needed another operation, but the surgeon refused to operate because of the state of her arteries. She would probably not survive the procedure.

Her blood pressure was a phenomenal 200/155. Asked about

this, Eileen commented it had 'always been rather high'! She had been taking drugs to control it for years.

Her husband tells the story:

> It was a lucky day for Eileen when she saw the article in *Here's Health* magazine about chelation therapy.
>
> She had already had an operation for a blockage at the lower end of her aorta some 11 years ago and when a similar problem presented itself last year a senior consultant thought a second operation was far too dangerous.
>
> I don't doubt that he was right, but it created a very traumatic situation which seemed insurmountable – until we saw the article. Fortunately tests showed she was suitable for treatment.
>
> Twelve months ago she could only walk, very slowly, for a few paces with the aid of a stick. She was unable to climb any stairs. Today she walks well, climbs steps and has even been dancing. An additional bonus is that she has been able to give up her blood pressure tablets – she has taken them for years – and her general feeling of well-being is a pleasure to see.

Staff at the Chelation Centre did not think that Eileen was going to get better, as several times she arrived for an infusion still hobbling with her stick. It turned out that, encouraged by her husband, between sessions she had been overdoing her newly-returned ability to walk and was actually suffering because her muscles were redeveloping.

At the end of her programme, the Centre's summary recorded her as looking, in her face, 15 years younger, able to walk more than a mile unaided 'and very gracefully', with her blood pressure stabilized at 135/80 and all drugs withdrawn.

'Thanks to chelation therapy', says her husband, 'Eileen has been given a new lease of life for which she and I are profoundly grateful.'

Another person with walking problems, whom we'll call Gerry, had a classic case of what is known as claudication, and it was so bad that he could only cover 25 yards before the pain stopped him.

Claudication literally means limping, or lameness. It usually turns up in people with circulatory problems as intermittent claudication. It is usually caused by the arteries being severely diseased. The pain starts up soon after walking, becomes so bad that the person has to stop, and then disappears completely when the legs are rested.

Gerry reports:

In January I could walk no farther than 25 yards and was in acute pain at the end of it. I would have to return to my car walking flat footed on my left foot because it was too painful to take weight on the ball of my foot. There was a gradual improvement in that by July I could walk 200 yards – but slowly and with a lot of pain.

I started chelation in July and noticed no improvement until the sixth infusion, when I realized one day that I had walked from Oxford Circus station to Wimpole Street with only marginal discomfort in the leg.

After the seventh infusion I found a considerable improvement again, and after the eighth I was able to walk *briskly*, and I recall telling Dr P and several of the patients that I had turned a corner. The improvement continued and I have now had 11 infusions.

Two days ago I walked one and a half miles (2.4km) at normal walking pace with no discomfort in the leg. I sat for a few minutes and did the return walk, at the end of which I had only marginal discomfort in the leg. Yesterday I set out on a *brisk* walk (service marching pace of four miles [6.4km] to the hour) without any problem.

My legs were marginally uncomfortable at the end of it, but what one has to remember is that years ago, before claudication became apparent, my legs, like those of other fit people, would have some mild degree of discomfort after a brisk one-and-a-half-mile walk.

As a means of testing chelation, Gerry purposely did not lose weight or stop smoking during the 11 infusions! 'The benefits I have seen could only have come from chelation,' he says. 'Now that I have conducted my own clinical trial, weight loss and cessation of smoking will be effected.'

Gerry also reported 'side-effects' – early improvements in fact: 'Better hearing, eyesight, mental alertness and erections.'

Another man who continued to smoke through his treatment worried James Kavanagh: 'He did not make as much progress as he might have done, and I was sure that his next step would be surgery.'

Michael (not his real name) had severe claudication when he first came for chelation. He had been unable to sleep properly for months, since as soon as he put his legs anywhere near the horizontal the pains in his calf became unbearable, since gravity was no longer able to help the flow of blood. He could walk only 100 yards (91m) before seizing up and had been forced to stop work. He looked very old.

The cause of his condition seemed to be his heavy smoking plus slightly high blood cholesterol readings. The tests showed severe circulatory disease in his legs, but no one could judge the exact extent of it since Michael was not about to let anyone cut into him. A professor at a leading London hospital had re-commended an invasive check of his lumbar area and he had refused. In fact he wasn't all that happy about chelation, and had seemed to agree to a course – twice a week for three months – only because he was more afraid that if things got worse he would *have* to agree to invasive investigations.

He was, in the consultant's terms, 'a real problem'. The Chelation Centre really thought he would need surgery, but Michael was set against it. The Doppler, sound-wave test used at the Centre revealed massive obstructions in his arteries. And he would not stop smoking.

Yet, against the expectations and against the odds, chelation was able to make a real impression in the three months. A revealing measure of the improvement was a walking treadmill test three months after completion of the initial course, which shows whether the improvement is lasting and is maintained. Michael initially stopped in pain at one minute 30 seconds at 2 mph (3.2kph) on the flat; his follow-up showed he could go for three minutes 50 seconds.

This added to the other effects: the night-time resting pain was relieved, and the Doppler test showed minor improvements in the flow of blood where previously there had been all the signs of an irreversible continuation of the blocking; these combined to relieve Michael of a great deal of anxiety.

James Kavanagh hoped that Michael's GP would be able to find the funds to enable him to take another course of treatment and would help him stop smoking, but could only be pleased at the results: 'He is able to walk and produce his own lactic acid (a by-product of exercise) to help himself and he now works full-time again. And he is much more happy and confident as a result.'

Another huge improvement in claudication was seen in a 54-year-old man we'll call Peter, who could manage a maximum of 150 yards (137m) on a slight incline before being stopped by the pain in his right calf. This is no way for a 54-year-old to face life.

This man, a flight engineer, had faced – and passed – regular flying medicals. They had not picked up, or looked for, the cause of his problem – a generalized arteriosclerosis of the right leg with blockages – which the Chelation Centre tests found out to be due to very high levels of cholesterol.

Peter had given up smoking years before, so it was clear that the dramatic improvement in his condition was again due only to chelation. Dramatic? Well, he had only ten infusions starting in November. When he booked in for his seventh infusion in March, he had already taken part in a *ten-mile* (16km) cross-country walk without any claudication pain.

After ten treatments, he was reporting that his walks on the Downs were back to the distances he was covering five years previously, walking a regular 4-5 miles (6.5-8km) with no pain.

Other ailments

Some people show their circulatory problems by not being able to walk too far; others are more dramatic – they pass out.

These are the 'cranial' cases. People with disease of the arteries that take blood and oxygen to the brain. On the way, the blood passes through the neck, and at the carotid arteries, the main highways from heart to head, Doppler sound testing can reveal where and how bad the obstructions are.

Luckily for the 'cranials', chelation can be as dramatic as their habit of falling over several times a day.

Catherine (not her real name) was 66 and was blacking out three or more times a day. This was not only embarrassing, but dangerous. If she felt herself 'going' at home she could usually avoid the corners of tables or 'arrange' to drop saucepans where they would do least damage, but she was rightly worried that she might collapse while out shopping and be hit by a car.

But it was an embarrassing moment that highlighted her condition at the Chelation Centre. The first thing staff knew about it was when she turned up for her first infusion and passed out in the toilet. Since then the locks have been changed so that they can be opened from the outside in emergencies.

The problem with cranial insufficiency is that you feel bad all over even when you're not falling over. The brain needs massive amounts of oxygen. When it doesn't get it you can feel washed out all the time, and generally ill every day for no good reason.

Catherine not only came across as a morose person, but looked ill, with a yellow/grey complexion. That was to clear by her fourteenth infusion, so that she looked totally normal. Much more satisfying – and quicker – was the fact that she had not a single collapse since her first infusion – a remarkable result.

The Doppler scans showed how her cranial circulation improved and she was so much happier in her outlook. And, said James Kavanagh with the 'before' and 'after' reports to hand: 'As with many cases, the kidney function improves with chelation treatment and this can assist well-being.'

The sound-wave scans are a popular, non-invasive tool. 'Around 75 per cent of people attending the Clinic come only for the Doppler exam,' said Kavanagh. 'Some exhibit a moderate/severe stroke risk.'

A lady we'll call Janice, aged 55, came into this category. She had already used surgery and the Gerson cancer therapy to deal successfully with three malignant melanomas three years before. Now the Doppler showed problems in her carotid arteries; follow-up tests showed the cause to be her high cholesterol level. Without effective preventive treatment she was a candidate for a sudden and severe loss of blood supply to the brain.

Janice has started a course of chelation confident that she can successfully rid her arteries of plaque and improve her health.

Eye improvement
FD, 67-year-old man. Rapid left eyesight degeneration over previous six months. This was said to be avascular, that is, in an area not reached by the bloodstream, and so untreatable by chelation.

But FD had been so astonished by his wife's health changes that he decided to try treatment himself, on the basis that all deposits and their dispersal, plus nerve regeneration depend on a good blood supply – and chelation would help bring that about.

Last report was that the deterioration seemed to have halted. A prominent eye specialist is reviewing the case.

Arthritis subsides
HW, 60-year-old woman. Despite operations for relief of

obstructions in the blood supply of her legs she had been in constant pain for many years. After the second infusion, she was able to spend most of the day on her feet without pain. Useful side-effects included the disappearance of varicose veins in her leg and an almost ¼ inch (7mm), six-year-old vein on her wrist.

A severe arterial thumping sound in the area of her ear became less noisy. Arthritis of her knuckles subsided to such an extent that she is now able to exert her full grip instead of being able to close her hand only partially.

After a stroke

KB, 57-year-old woman. Stroke nine years previously had left her with considerable paralysis still on her right side. The Doppler sound scan showed an impaired blood flow in the carotid arteries at the neck, and this was corrected with six infusions.

With this restored blood supply, nerve regeneration becomes possible and she was recommended to start physiotherapy.

Record run

AP, 40-year-old man. Previous investigations of his heart involved catheterization, passing a tube into the heart to try to find out what is going on. This apparently revealed severe 'blockages' and he had been offered bypass surgery.

During chelation his chest pains gradually abated and he finally proved he was 100 per cent fit in great style: following his twelfth infusion he ran, complete with overcoat and overnight bag, via two underground trains to catch a train at Victoria station within 14 minutes of leaving the Clinic. It was 'an amazing performance', say staff. He arrived puffed, but without pain.

Mucus problem clears – after 30 years

SK, 58-year-old man. There was a gradual improvement in his angina after the fourth infusion, and there were valuable side-effects. His eyesight improved and, most surprisingly, after only the second infusion a serious nasal mucus discharge ceased. This had been going on for 30 years, since he had received a blow on the head.

The Doppler readings on his carotid arteries support his own reports of progress and he is now completely free of all drugs.

Never too late?

TS, 82-year-old woman. She could only walk one block due to intermittent claudication. She had coeliac disease (allergy to gluten, the protein found in wheat) and severe potassium loss. Her kidney function was impaired and as a result she had to be given only a half-dosage of EDTA for the first five sessions – long enough for this to improve.

Her kidneys now perform better and she walks double the distance. Just as delightful to the Clinic staff, she recovered her sparkling personality and outgoing nature, 'suspected but not seen before to such an entertaining degree'.

IB, 72-year-old woman. Angina and intermittent claudication disappeared after eight treatments despite extreme cold weather in London after the warmth of her native Trinidad. She spent most of her days visiting and shopping in London, rather than resting. Eyesight problems of occasional black 'floaters' stopped after the second infusion.

Avoiding the bypass

RB, 40-year-old man. Crushed by angina, although suffering only occasional attacks, he was offered a coronary bypass operation. An athletics coach, and aware of the benefits of treating the whole body rather than isolated parts, he opted for chelation.

Residual angina proved to have gone after no further pains occurred for two weeks following the fourteenth infusion.

Putting back the sparkle

BP, 55-year-old woman. Her ankles were swollen after only little walking. She was overweight although she ate very little and felt generally 'two degrees under', with lack of energy.

The Doppler test showed only slight abnormalities in cerebral arteries. Following ten infusions, the water retention in her ankles cleared up. She has lost one and a half stones (9.5kg) and has regained a real sparkle to herself, much remarked on by friends.

Chapter 8

Diet and exercise during (and after) chelation therapy

There is very little point in having a series of chelation treatments if the person thus improved is not going to take advantage of the improved circulatory capacity which it provides. This should be seen as a second chance, an opportunity to keep things right and to prevent the inevitable deterioration which would take place if the same old habits of eating, life-style and exercise were followed.

The tragedy of much of the heroic effort which goes into surgical intervention for cardiovascular disease is that it touches on just a part of a severely compromised system. What is the long-term point or value of bypassing a blocked region with an unclogged vein or artery if the rest of the channels are already somewhat damaged and if little is done to alter those habits and patterns which led to the clogging in the first place? What value a new heart if the system it is pumping blood through is silted up?

When chelation unclogs circulatory obstructions this affects almost the entire system, and a host of factors which could rapidly set the degenerative ball rolling again if they remained behind, such as heavy metals and low density lipoproteins, are removed from the body along with the metastatic calcium. Even then it would be but a short-term improvement if the underlying habits which led to the degenerative changes were not addressed, whether these involve lack of exercise, poor stress-coping abilities, smoking and alcohol abuse, dietary imbalances, toxic encumbrances or any combination of these and other causes.

The changes needed to keep the new-found circulatory improvement (after EDTA or surgery) are the very ones which would have prevented the circulatory decline in the first place and can be broadly divided into the eating pattern followed and the many factors in the person's life which lead so inevitably to arterial damage and all that follows.

Those elements which need to be seriously considered include:

- Changing dietary habits.
- Providing specific nutrient aids.
- Increasing aerobic activity.
- Decreasing exposure to smoke, alcohol and toxins.
- Learning stress-proofing techniques.

A prescription for a healthy heart is a prescription for good health generally. All the same features are present and these are now so well established that it almost seems not worth repeating the same 'rules'. However, cardiovascular health is in such an appalling state that those who know, and hopefully follow, most of the healthy-heart guidelines will hopefully forgive a brief repetition of the most important points.

Diet

Fats

A great deal of agreement exists (a rare thing in science and even rarer in medicine) as to what needs to be done in dietary terms to meet the needs of the cardiovascular system in a modern world. Expert committees have deliberated and come to clear decisions on matters such as the need for a reduction overall in the amount of fat that is eaten.

The average West European and American eats anything up to (and sometimes beyond) 40 per cent of their total energy intake from fats, much of which is of the undesirable saturated type. Various health authorities such as the Senate Committee and NACNE in the UK advise reducing this to between 30 and 35 per cent.

Nathan Pritikin, the revolutionary health expert who developed a diet and exercise programme for cardiovascular dysfunction (Pritikin, 1980), advised reducing this to a miniscule 10 per cent.

Elmer Cranton suggests that a more easily attainable (although still difficult) target is 20 per cent, virtually cutting fat and oil intake in half with the majority of this in the form of polyunsaturated and mono-unsaturated (olive oil) forms.

In practical terms this means avoiding fat on meat and avoiding most meat derived from pigs, cows or sheep as well as skin of poultry. This leaves game, poultry apart from skin, and fish as sources of animal protein for those who do not wish to adopt a vegetarian mode of eating. Game has a fat level of less than 4 per cent as a rule (some beef contains up to 30 per cent fat) and this is usually high in polyunsaturated or mono-unsaturated fats compared with the less desirable saturated form found in dairy produce and domesticated animal meat.

This highlights an important message: not all oils and fats are bad for cardiovascular health, indeed some are vital. We need essential fatty acids in our diet (hence the word essential in their title) and we can learn a good deal by looking at the dietary habits of people who live in regions (such as the Mediterranean basin) where heart disease is a rarity. Among the important differences in their diet is a very high intake of mono-unsaturated oil (olive), which has been shown to have a cholesterol lowering effect. They also eat abundant fish, a major source of eicosapentenoic acid, a protective factor for the cardiovascular system (and of course garlic which reduces the adhesiveness – stickiness – of blood platelets). Another Mediterranean bonus is the eating of the herb purslane, a rich source of gamma linoleic acid (also found abundantly in linseed) and an important source of essential fatty acids. Inclusion of these factors – garlic, fish (especially cold water varieties), linseed and olive oil instead of other salad oils – all act to protect the heart and its functions.

No frying or roasting of food should be done and dairy produce – apart from skimmed milk and very low-fat yogurt or cottage cheese – should be avoided.

Eggs

Approximately one person in five is affected by a rise in blood levels of cholesterol after eating eggs. The other four show little or no change in their cholesterol levels after eating normal quantities of egg. It should be realized that most cholesterol (which is an essential part of every cell of the body) is made in the body, unrelated to dietary intake of the substance but influenced by such factors as overall fat intake, sugar intake, smoking and, in some instances, coffee intake. The moderate eating of eggs (three or four per week) seems therefore to be without danger for most people.

Carbohydrates and sugars

Cardiovascular health is improved when refined carbohydrates play only a very limited part in the diet. This means substituting wholegrain for white flour products and white rice. Wholegrain products, brown pasta, bread and rice are readily available and contain high levels of fibre which helps clear excess cholesterol from the intestines (especially oats), as well as providing essential vitamins, minerals and trace elements, which are largely or entirely removed in any refining process.

At present we in the West eat around 45 per cent of our food as carbohydrate, with an average of half of this as refined sugars and flour products. The expert guidelines suggest that we should increase carbohydrates to around 58 per cent of our diet, but with the simple sugars, etc., declining to no more than 15 per cent of our dietary intake.

'Complex carbohydrates' are the major nutrients contained in vegetables and fruits, nuts, seeds and beans, and of course whole grains (milled but not refined). So a diet which emphasizes vegetables at both main meals with brown rice, pasta and/or bread, as well as abundant use of fresh nuts and seeds (sunflower, sesame, pumpkin, linseed, etc.) and the members of the bean family (lentils, chickpeas, etc.), as well as fresh fruit – to the extent that these foods account for just under two thirds of the total food eaten – is the target we are set.

No wonder vegetarians have such fine cardiovascular health.

Protein

As described under the heading *Fats*, the types of animal protein most likely to assist in achieving the aims being set are game, poultry (minus its skin) and fish. In the USA and UK an average intake of around 12 per cent of total energy consists of protein, and this is thought to be a reasonable level.

A useful strategy to enhance heart health would be if this 12 per cent were made up of more vegetable sources of protein (pulses, for example) and less from animal sources. Again, the example can be given of the vegetarian who combines nuts and grains, or pulses (bean family) and grains, for their protein content, and who have an infinitely better degree of cardiovascular function than do meat eaters.

Fibre

Eating a diet rich in complex carbohydrates ensures adequate fibre, which is necessary for cholesterol clearance from the digestive tract. Not all fibres are the same, however: oat bran acts quite differently (in cholesterol mopping terms, that is) from wheat bran (see Chapter 12). Authorities in the West urge that we eat up to 30 grams of fibre daily, with half of this from cereals and the rest from fruits and vegetables. In rural Africa (where cardiovascular disease is rare) the intake of fibre is anything up to 150 grams daily. Interestingly, when people from the African countryside migrate to cities and adopt a diet low in fibre their cardiovascular health declines rapidly.

The best cholesterol-lowering fibres are found in oats, fruits and vegetables and the leading providers are: blackberries, bananas, apricots, apples, raspberries, prunes, passion fruit, damsons, haricot beans, bean sprouts, broccoli, cabbage, carrots, celery, lentils, mushrooms, peas and potatoes.

Alcohol
This is an area of some debate, with a very small amount of alcohol (1½ glasses of wine or 1 pint of beer daily) being shown to enhance cardiovascular function (but with some negative effect on liver function) and anything more than that amount having negative effects. Overall health experts agree that alcohol is undesirable but that these limits are fairly safe.

Coffee
The drinking of boiled coffee in any quantity has been shown to increase levels of cholesterol in the blood.

Salt
Because of its known association with increased blood pressure (a major factor in cardiovascular degeneration), salt intake should be reduced dramatically from its current level of around 12 grams daily to no more than 3 grams per day per person, none of which should be added at table. It is now known that damage from salt starts when we are very young and if children can be taught to enjoy unsalted food they could be saved a good deal of distress later in life.

Dietary pattern

So what would a typical day's diet on such a pattern look like?

Breakfast
Nut/seed and dried-fruit mixture, plus live low-fat yogurt, or
Wholegrain cereal plus (live) low-fat yogurt, or
Oatmeal porridge, or
Wholemeal toast with vegetarian margarine and sugarless
   jam
Fresh fruit
Egg (alternate days)
Drink of herbal tea (unsweetened)

Mid-morning/afternoon
Herbal tea or fresh fruit or handful of seeds and fresh nuts

Lunch/supper
One of these meals could comprise game, poultry or fish,
plus a variety of fresh vegetables and a side salad, plus
wholemeal bread and fresh fruit.
The other meal could include pasta (wholemeal) or rice
with homemade tomato sauce, or
A rice and pulse (lentil, etc.) dish, plus stir-fried vegetables,
or
A mixed salad with jacket potato and low-fat cheese, etc.
For dessert, fresh fruit or low-fat yogurt.

Imagination and some effort are all that limit the application of
this type of eating pattern with its attendant benefits to
cardiovascular health.

Supplements

There are a number of areas which we should consider if we
wish to improve cardiovascular status via supplementation.
One involves antioxidant (anti-free radical) activity and another
the balancing and normalizing of any imbalances in mineral
status (potassium/sodium or calcium/magnesium, for example). There is also the way in which some supplemented
substances (such as the enzyme derived from the pineapple
plant – bromelaine) can specifically reduce platelet adhesiveness, as well as very important protective effects from certain
of the individual amino acids (building blocks of protein) which
have recently been researched.

- The anti-oxidant vitamins, minerals, enzymes and amino acids are all capable of being supplemented in order to improve the deactivation of free radical activity and the detoxification of heavy metals and other toxins. Research evidence abounds as to the relative protection of cardio-vascular function (and general health) achieved when these factors are in good supply in the diet, whether through food or as added extras in the form of nutritional supplements.

  Without analysing the particular ways in which these act (see Chapter 4 on free radicals) these can best be taken in combinations such as vitamins A, C, E and the mineral selenium. If taken individually, daily doses which can give antioxidant protection are:

  Beta carotene (which the body turns into vitamin A)

50,000 IU
Vitamin C	1-3 grams
Vitamin E	200-400 IU
Selenium	200 micrograms
Cysteine (amino acid)	1.5 grams

  As an additional background aid the taking of a modest level of the B-complex group of vitamins is suggested. Find a formulation which provides not less than 25 milligrams each of the major B vitamins (thiamine, pyridoxine, etc.) and if you are a big meat eater take in addition (at a separate time of day to the B-complex) 100 milligrams of pyridoxine (B6) to help protect the arteries from damage from break-down products of the high-protein intake.

- Balancing minerals status is an individual matter, depending very much on what imbalances are present. A general 'insurance' supplement of calcium/magnesium containing twice as much calcium as magnesium is usually suggested (1 gram calcium/.5 gram magnesium).

  In addition a general mineral supplement which contains zinc (around 20 milligrams), manganese (20 milligrams), potassium (100 milligrams), chromium (200 micrograms) and molybdenum (100 micrograms), but *no* iron or copper is suggested.

  Many authorities advocate magnesium supplementation on its own (i.e., without additional calcium) at doses of up to 800 milligrams daily, especially for those with ischaemic heart disease (angina symptoms). Magnesium is frequently given intraveneously for people severely compromised by angina-type symptoms during the course of chelation therapy.

- Oil of evening primrose (500-1000 milligrams daily) supplies essential fatty acids and becomes increasingly important as we get older. Of course if enough linseed (ideal addition to breakfast cereal) or purslane (delicious on salad) is eaten, supplementation is unnecessary. The all-important eicosapentenoic acid derived from cold-water fish is a useful aid to cardiovascular health (3-6 EPA capsules) and should be taken unless the individual is a vegetarian or eats a good deal (twice weekly) of appropriate fish.

The pineapple plant extract bromelaine is also useful for similar purposes in doses of up to 1000 milligrams daily.

For those who do not enjoy eating garlic, the oil of this amazing bulb can be taken in capsule form ad lib.

Even more powerful at reducing platelet aggregation is ginger (*Zingebar officinale*) and if it is difficult to incorporate this into the diet in any quantity, it too can be found in capsule form (dried powdered ginger).

- Two amino acids have been shown to have remarkable abilities to assist cardiovascular function:

1 Carnitine: needed more by men than women, this has been shown to assist enormously in conditions such as intermittent claudication and as a protector against myocardial infarction. It also has the ability to mobilize and remove fat deposits. People who have had an infarction have been shown to have a gross deficiency of this amino acid in the muscles of the heart itself.

For best absorption supplementation of individual amino acids is always taken away from meal times, with water only and perhaps a small quantity of carbohydrate (e.g., a bite of bread). Doses are usually between 1 and 1.5 grams daily, in two or three divided doses.

2 Taurine: this too is usually deficient in cardiac tissue when a crisis occurs. It has the ability to 'spare' potassium which is absolutely vital to normal cardiovascular function. Another feature of taurine's function is its ability to keep cholesterol soluble in the bile, thus aiding in its elimination. It can usefully be supplemented in cases of intermittent claudication and cardiovascular distress in doses of be-

tween 0.5 and 1 gram daily (away from meal times and any other amino acids).

● Methionine is used to help detoxify heavy metals and is a powerful antioxidant. The body can make either taurine or carnitine out of methionine and this makes it a useful general supplement. People who develop atherosclerosis are commonly found to have low levels of methionine in the bloodstream. Doses of .5 to 1 gram daily are suggested for general protection (away from meal times and other amino acids).

Exercise

There can be few people in our society who are not at least slightly aware of aerobic exercise, although it is clear that not too many actually understand what it is all about.

Dr Kenneth Cooper, the American physician who developed the system, conceived of being able to teach anyone, starting from a point of any degree of fitness or unfitness, to exercise safely in such a way as to be able to achieve a steadily increasing degree of enhanced cardiovascular and respiratory function.

Obviously no one who has cardiovascular disease should start aerobic activity without an all-clear from their medical adviser, but the work of both Cooper (1980) and Nathan Pritikin (1980) has demonstrated beyond doubt that almost no matter how advanced the damage there remains something that can be done via exercise to improve matters. The beginner may well need to be under supervision and guidance, since it is essential to learn to monitor the effects on the heart rate of whatever form of exercise is being performed. True aerobic exercise demands that a basic level of increased heart (pulse) rate be achieved and that this be maintained for not less than 20 (ideally 30) minutes three times weekly with no more than a day between such efforts. It is equally essential that an upper 'safe' limit be established beyond which there would be danger of straining the heart.

As Colin Goodliffe (1987) explains:

The heart has a maximum level of activity and output which it would be dangerous to exceed. This is the upper limit of the range which must be achieved in cardiovascular exercise.

There is also a level of heart effort which it is necessary to reach, if any good at all is to be achieved and this is the lower level of the heart rate which must be aimed for during exercise.

We will explain how to discover what these two figures are for you later in this chapter. First, however, it is important that we establish the aerobic/chelation connection.

Exercise helps chelation

In Chapter 2 we saw that chelation processes are continuous throughout life and are an essential part of most body processes. When the muscles work they produce lactic acid as a breakdown product and lactic acid is almost as powerful a chelating agent as acetic acid. As long as strong and rapid muscular activity is continuing, so will lactic acid continue to circulate in high quantities, chelating undesirable substances all the while.

Dr Johan Bjorksten (1974) explains:

> Lactic acid is not as effective as EDTA in its speed but given enough time to act it seems comparable in total removal of chelatable metals. It [lactic acid] is a fair to good chelating agent which is present in almost double quantities during the time of moderate muscular exertion, and which declines to normal levels abruptly in a few minutes upon cessation of the muscular action.

Sustained exercise patterns (walking, jogging, running, skiing, swimming, etc.) are therefore seen to offer this natural chelation benefit. Bjorksten sees this as providing a basis for increased longevity, while Walker and Gordon (1982) make the important point that: 'the duration of muscular exertion is more important than its intensity in order to achieve a chelating effect from exercise'.

Chelation quenches free radicals

Cranton and Frackelton (1982) point out another remarkable function of enhanced oxygenation brought on by aerobic activity:

> Proper oxygenation enhances defences against free radicals. Aerobic exercise stimulates blood flow and improves oxygen utilization resulting in adequate oxygenation to remote

capillary beds. When conditions of health exist oxygen acts as a free radical scavenger during exercise and reduces free radical pathology.

Working out your 'aerobic fitness index'

It is considered that the fastest the human heart can beat without extreme danger is 220 beats per minute.

In order to establish your particular fitness index (the low and high rates needed for safe and effective aerobic exercise) we start with this number 220 from which we deduct your present age, which we can state hypothetically to be 50:

$$220 - 50 = 170$$

From this number we also deduct your resting morning pulse rate. For three successive mornings, check your pulse on waking – before getting out of bed or eating or drinking anything, even water.

Let us say this rate is 70:

$$170 - 70 = 100$$

We now need to establish what 60 per cent and 80 per cent of this final figure are:

60 per cent of 100 = 60
80 per cent of 100 = 80

To these two figures we add back your morning pulse rate, giving us:

60 + 70 = 130
80 + 70 = 150

These are the figures of your current aerobic fitness index *if you are 50 years old and if your morning resting pulse is 70.*

In order to achieve benefit to your cardiovascular system you need to get your pulse rate above 130 and maintain it there for not less than 20, and ideally 30, minutes three times per week with no more than a day between each aerobic effort.

If, however, your pulse rate were to exceed 150 during these efforts you would be in danger of stressing the heart.

It is best to check the pulse rate for 15 seconds every 5 to 7 minutes during exercise (and to multiply by 4 for the rate per minute) and thereafter, if necessary, to increase the amount of effort or speed of effort (if the rate was below the lower figure) or to slow down if it was above the higher figure.

When you have been performing aerobic exercises for some weeks it is a good idea to recheck the morning pulse rate, for as you get fitter this will slow down, giving you a new set of aerobic index figures (obviously this also alters as you get older).

Example

Dr Cooper (1980) gives examples of general exercise such as walking (undoubtedly the safest after swimming), in which a moderate level of fitness would be achieved progressively over a 16-week period. This is based on walking a specific distance in a particular time, which gradually gets shorter, requiring more effort. Each of the times/distances listed is meant to be walked not less than five times in any given week.

In week 1, a mile (1.6 km) is walked in 15 minutes (5 times in the week).

In week 2, a mile is walked in 14 minutes.

In week 3, a mile is walked in 13 mins 45 seconds.

In weeks 4, 5 and 6, 1½ miles (2.4 km) is walked in 21 mins 30 seconds.

In week 7, two miles (3.2 km) is walked in 28 minutes.

In week 8, two miles is walked in 27 mins 45 seconds.

In weeks 9 and 10, two miles is walked in 27 mins 30 seconds.

In week 11, 2½ miles (4 km) is walked in 35 minutes.

In week 12, 2½ miles is walked in 34 mins 30 seconds.

In weeks 13, 14 and 15, 3 miles (4.8 km) is walked in 42 minutes.

In week 16, 4 miles (6.4 km) is walked in 56 minutes.

Thereafter this last timing and distance, using the pulse rate to monitor whether enough effort is being used to maintain fitness.

If anyone were starting this 16-week programme from a position of relatively poor fitness the times given for each distance would be used as a guide only and the pulse would be taken several times during the walk to see whether speed of walking was enough to achieve the lower figure on the aerobic fitness index (if not, walking faster is called for), or if it was above the higher figure, in which case slowing down would be the obvious move.

Aerobic exercise, ideally accompanied by gentle stretching

exercises to warm up and with a degree of gentle movement to 'warm down' is safe and effective in enhancing chelation therapy or for enhancing cadiovascular function on its own.

Always check with your physician/health adviser before starting new forms of exercise.

And what of the mind?

Cardiovascular ill-health has long been linked with the effects of stress and anxiety. It should go without saying that the mind and body are a unit and that unless those negative factors arising out of poor stress-coping strategies or negative emotions are dealt with, a complete degree of recovery of cardiovascular (or any other area of) health is unlikely. Exercise itself has powerful beneficial effects on the mind and emotions. Along with nutritional and aerobic efforts, it is suggested that efforts be directed towards stress reduction using the extensive knowledge now available as to the value of regularly employed relaxation and meditation methods.

Smoking

Smoking of any sort imposes unbearable strain on cardiovascular function. It increases the body level of cadmium (a highly toxic heavy metal) appreciably and is a major cause of free radical activity. It reduces necessary oxygen intake and is probably the single greatest underlying life-style habit which contributes to and/or aggravates disease of the heart and circulatory system. It is plainly an indefensible habit and those physicians who simply refuse to treat patients with such health problems until they stop smoking are a growing band. Anyone having chelation therapy and who continues to smoke is plainly afflicted by a death wish.

Chapter 9

Oral chelation

Oral chelation simply means trying to use foods or substances taken by mouth to chelate undesirable substances out of the body. There are two basic approaches: the first uses foods and nutrient supplements to achieve this effect and the other uses oral EDTA supplements.

Does it work?

We will discuss the controversial oral EDTA approach after first looking at the nutritional approach.

The current vogue for oat-based foods as a means of reducing cholesterol levels is but one form of chelation which we take for granted. In fact the different forms of fibre found in food, soluble pectin in apples and other fruits, guar in beans as well as the forms found in grains, all produce multiple chelating effects as they pass through the system. These act largely in the bowel where they speed up transit time and in this way prevent cholesterol reabsorption from bile as well as clearing putrefactive material from the system more rapidly. Fats in the bloodstream are reduced by soluble fibre in the diet, reducing the potential for free radical activity.

The advice given in Chapter 8 regarding the ideal pattern of eating can easily produce just these effects if followed reasonably closely. In addition many basic nutrients such as vitamins C and E are natural chelators and when in abundant supply act in the bloodstream to damp down free radical activity as well as chelating toxic substances.

Several formulae have been developed for oral chelation using variable combinations of substances. Some are extremely complex and others simple enough to put together, given a little patience and effort.

Oral chelation: Formula 1

This is known as the Rinse Formula, after Dr Jacobus Rinse of Vermont, who has popularized this highly effective combination of substances, now advocated by the Dutch National Health Board for the prevention of heart disease
A daily intake of the following is suggested:

- 4 grams of lecithin (try to ensure a form which is high in phosphatidyl choline)
- 12 grams of coarsely chopped sunflower seeds (for their linoleic acid, potassium and fibre content)
- 5 grams debittered Brewer's yeast powder for its selenium, chromium and B vitamins (not suggested for anyone with active Candida albicans overgrowth)
- 2 grams of bone-meal as a source of calcium and magnesium, or a nutritional supplement form of calcium and magnesium (in a ratio of 2:1)
- 5 grams unpasteurized or untreated wheatgerm for its vitamin E and trace elements
- 500 milligrams of vitamin C (as sodium ascorbate, in powder form if possible)
- 100IU vitamin E (make sure this is D-Alpha tocopherol)
- 40 milligrams vitamin B6 (pyridoxine)
- 20-30 milligrams zinc (picolinate or orotate)

Blend these ingredients together in a food processor and keep refrigerated until use.

The amounts given are for *daily* consumption (around 30 grams in total) and it is probably wise to make up enough for a few weeks at a time and to keep this well covered and chilled until it is consumed, as breakfast or with any meal.
    Research at the University of Alabama by Drs C Butterworth and C Krumdieck (published in 1974 in the *American Journal of Clinical Nutrition*) has shown that the combination of linoleic acid and lecithin, as well as the other nutrients such as vitamin C, act to form an enzyme Lecithin-Cholesterol-Acyl-Transferase (LCAT), which chelates cholesterol deposits from arterial walls at normal body temperatures. These foods are suggested by Dr Rinse as a means of ensuring that the raw materials for

formation of LCAT are readily available.

Oral chelation: Formula 2

Dr Kurt Donsbach, the dynamic and controversial author of dozens of health booklets and pamphlets, and director of an 'holistic medical clinic in California, has provided a chelation formula for oral use (Chelation pamphlet 1985, published by the author). He states:

> Oral chelation is probably a misnomer, since the formulation does not attach itself to, or eliminate via the urine, the calcium in the bloodstream as does the EDTA form of intravenous chelation. The term is used because the end-result is the same, with considerably less discomfort and cost (approximately 1500 per cent less).
>
> The two chelation approaches, intravenous infusion of EDTA and the oral nutrient approach, both are lifesavers to countless individuals. Many physicians are now opting for a combination of the two methods since they work in different fashions and by doing so find that the intravenous infusions can be cut down from a series of 30 to only 10 treatments. Furthermore, by using a maintenance dose of the oral, the patient is protected for the future so that he does not need to be rechelated with EDTA.

John Stirling, an Australian research scientist working in the UK, compares oral and intravenous chelation (although he is discussing oral use of EDTA, not oral nutritional chelation) with intravenous EDTA (Stirling, 1989):

> I would opt for intravenous over oral EDTA in extreme life-threatening situations. Intravenous is more direct obviously, and results can be noticed sooner, and the cost variance is considerable.

So what does Dr Donsbach suggest as oral chelation? A great deal, as the following shows:

Vitamin A (fish liver oil and beta carotene)	25,000IU
Vitamin D (fish liver oil)	400IU
Vitamin E	600IU
Vitamin C	3000mg
Vitamin B1	200mg

Vitamin B2	50mg
Vitamin B6	150mg
Niacin (B3)	100mg
Pantothenic acid (B5)	250mg
Vitamin B12	250mcg
Folic acid	400mcg
Biotin	100mcg
Choline	750mg
Inositol	100mg
PABA	150mg
Calcium carbonate	400mg
Magnesium oxide	500mg
Iodine (kelp)	225mcg
Copper gluconate	250mcg
Zinc gluconate	25mg
Potassium citrate and chloride	400mg
Manganese gluconate	10mg
Chromium	200mcg
Thymus extract	50mg
Spleen extract	50mg
Cod liver oil (EPA)	50mg
Hawthorn berry	25mg
Selenium	200mcg
Cysteine HCl	750mg
Methionine	200mg

Quite clearly, it is beyond the means of most people to compile a collection of nutrients which would meet these precise requirements. The particular formula given above is available in the USA from health stores. Anyone trying to put together an approximation of this suggested pattern could ask for assistance from a health store assistant who would doubtless, with a little effort, be able to combine a number of standard formulations and individual items towards this end.

It must be said that the combination put together by Dr Donsbach seems heroic in its complexity and although he explains precisely why each item is included, there remains a faint suggestion of 'shot-gun' supplementation in which the more things thrown together the greater the chance that something might do some good. The author provides this formulation as a matter of accuracy rather than as a strongly recommended course. My preference would be for something along the lines of Dr Rinse's formulation or the using of individual nutrient supplementation as outlined in Chapter 8.

Before we examine the use of oral EDTA, a reminder is in order at this point of the value of exercise as a chelation generating method. It is clear from Nathan Pritikin's work (Pritikin, 1980) that a combination of diet and exercise can do as much as chelation therapy in normalizing circulatory dysfunction; and remember that without attention to these areas chelation therapy will produce results which will not be sustained.

Lactic acid from muscle effort – a natural chelator

Dr Johan Bjorksten (1981) states: 'Lactic acid is not as effective as EDTA in speed, but given enough time to act, it seems comparable in total removal of chelatable metal.'

To achieve this effect, lactic acid levels have to be raised regularly and for sustained periods via endurance exercise patterns such as walking, swimming, cycling, etc. This must not be confused with aerobic exercise in which specific cardio-vascular training is taking place only if a specific degree of effort is sustained (see Chapter 8 on aerobic principles). In order to achieve the lactic acid chelating effect it is more important that *duration* (time spent exercising) is focused on rather than *degree* of effort.

A combination of Dr Rinse's formula and regular exercise offers a means of self-chelation of quite considerable sophistication.

However, when we speak of oral chelation it is to oral EDTA that we should really be looking.

EDTA as an oral supplement

A leading British firm supplies practitioners with their EDTA Complex supplement, which is based on a formula originally used in the clinic of Dr Josef Issels in West Germany and later used extensively in Australia by biologist and naturopath John Stirling.

Stirling says:

EDTA is usually degraded in the stomach and when given

orally is of little value, with approximately only 5 per cent being absorbed. However, when granulated and enteric coated, then pressed into a tablet and coated again, the absorption factor is almost 100 per cent.

This company is presently accumulating anecdotal evidence for the effectiveness of EDTA Complex. The tablets contain 150 mg of ethylene diamine-tetra-acetic acid with 100 mg of vitamin C and 100 IU of vitamin E. Suggested dose is one tablet morning and night, with food.

Stirling recommends it as a strong supportive agent along with diet and a correct organic mineral replacement therapy:

> The major advantage of using low-dose EDTA orally is that it is non-invasive, does not require electrolyte monitoring as the IV form does, and can be used as a long-term method to slowly remove toxic metals and arterial plaque from the system.

Stirling is also in favour of the oral form because he prefers to avoid any possibility of toxic overload on the kidneys and liver, the main organs of elimination that are used in taking chelated material out of the body.

Kidney function is not upset by this approach any more than it is in intravenous applications, and if there are concerns regarding kidney function this should be monitored during any course of treatment. No electrolyte imbalances have been observed with oral use of EDTA and diarrhoea is rarely a side-effect.

EDTA was given orally to patients, by the late Dr Issels at his cancer clinic in Germany, where it proved 'very useful'.

It is now being used in the UK by leading 'holistic' dentists, such as Jack Levenson, who wish to chelate mercury out of the system after it has entered via the amalgam fillings of the patient. In such cases an antioxidant formulation (vitamins A, C, E, etc.) as well as enzymes such as Glutathione peroxidase are supplemented along with oral EDTA. This form of EDTA should be seen as a form of maintenance rather than having the potential for chelation held by intravenous infusion. EDTA supplements for maintenance use are given morning and evening with food – doses of 150 mg are usual.

References and further reading

ANGHILERI, L. *et al.* (1976) Cell coat and tumour cells – effects of trypsin and EDTA *Oncology* 33: 17-23

ARONSON, A. *et al.* (1968) Studies with calcium EDTA in calves: toxicity and use in bovine lead poisoning *Tox. Appl. Pharm.* 12: 337-49

BARBER, A. and BERNHEIM, F. Lipid peroxidation: its measurement, occurrence and significance in animal tissue *Advances Gerent Research* 2: 355-403

BECHTEL, J. *et al.* (1956) The ECG effects of hypocalcaemia induced in normal subjects with edathamil disodium *Circulation* 13: 837-42

BELKNAP, E. (1952) EDTA in treatment of lead poisoning *Industrial Med. Surg.* 21 (6): 305-6

BERENSON, G. (1961) Studies of 'ground substance' of vessel wall and alterations in atherosclerosis and related diseases *Journal of Atherosclerosis Research* 1: 386-93

BERENSON, G. *et al.* (1974) 'Mucupolysaccharide-lipoprotein complexes in atherosclerosis' in *Arterial Mesenchyme and Arteriosclerosis* (eds. Wagner and Clarkson), Plenum Press, New York, pp.141-59.

BIRK, R. and RUPE, C. (1966) Treatment of systemic sclerosis with disodium EDTA, pyridoxine and reserpine *Henry Ford Hospital Bulletin* 14: 109-18

BJORKSTEN, J. (1974) 'Crosslinking and the ageing process' in *Theoretical Aspects of Ageing* (ed. M. Rockstein), Academic Press, New York

BJORKSTEN, J. (1981) *Longevity: A Quest* Bjorksten Research Foundation, Madison, Wisconsin

BLUMEN, W. and REICH, T. (1980) Leaded gasoline – a cause of cancer *Environment International* 3: 465-71 (Pergamon Press)

BOYLE, A. *et al.* (1961) Chelation therapy in circulatory and sclerosing diseases *Fed. Proc.* 29 (3) Part II, Suppl. 10: 243-51

BRODMAN, K. *et al.* (1949) The Cornell Medical Index: an adjunct to medical interview *J.A.M.A.* 140 (6): 530-34

BUTLER, A. (1952) Use of calcium EDTA in treating heavy-metal poisoning *Arch. Indust. Hygiene Occ. Med.* 7: 137-47

CLARKE, N. (1960) Atherosclerosis occlusive vascular disease and EDTA *American Journal of Cardiology* 6 (2): 233-6

CLARKE, N. *et al.* (1956) Treatment of angina pectoris with disodium EDTA *American Journal of Med. Sci.* 232: 654-66

*COOPER, K. (1980) *Aerobics* Bantam Books, New York

*CRANTON, E. and BRECHER, A. (1984) *Bypassing Bypass* Medex Publishing, Herndon, Virginia

*CRANTON, E. and FRACKELTON, J. (1982) Current status of EDTA chelation therapy *Journal of Holistic Medicine* 4: 24-33

CRAVEN, P. *et al.* (1975) Chelation Therapy *West Journal Med.* 122: 277-8

DEMOPOULOS, H. *et al.* (1982) Development of secondary pathology with free radical reactions as a threshold mechanism *J. Am. Col. Tox.* 2 (3): 173-84

DONSBACH, K. (1985) *Oral Chelation Therapy* International Institute of Natural Health Sciences, Huntington Beach, California

DUDLEY, H. *et al.* (1955) Pathological changes associated with use of sodium EDTA in treatment of hypercalcaemia *N.E.J. Med.* 252: 331-7

FOREMAN, H. *et al.* (1954) Use of calcium EDTA in cases of lead intoxication *Arch. Indust. Med.* 7: 148-51

FOREMAN, H. *et al.* (1956) Nephrotoxic hazard from uncontrolled adamethic calcium-disodium therapy *J.A.M.A.* 160 (12): 1042-6

FURST, A. (1960) 'Chelation and cancer – a speculative review' in *Metal Binding in Medicine* (eds M. J. Stevens and L. A. Johnson), J. B. Lippencott Co, Philadelphia, pp.336-349

GALLAGHER, C. (1960) *Nature,* 9 July, 162-4

GASIC, G. and GASIC, T. (1962) Removal and regeneration of cell coating in tumour cells *Nature,* p.196

*GOODLIFFE, C. (1987) *How to Avoid Heart Disease* Blandford Press

GOSLING, R. and KING, D. (1978) Processing arterial Doppler signals for clinical data *Handbook of Clinical Ultrasound* (eds de Vliegar *et al.*) John Wiley

*HALSTEAD, B. (1979) *The Scientific Basis of EDTA Chelation Therapy* Golden Quill Press, Colton, California

JICK, S. and KARSH, R. (1959) Effect of calcium chelation on cardiac arrhythmias and conduction disturbances *American J. of Cardiology* 4: 287-93

KAY, D. *et al.* (1984) Therapeutic effects of ascorbic acid and EDTA in manic depressive psychosis *Psychological Medicine* 14: 522-9

KIRK, J. E. (1965) The glutamic dehydrogenase and glutathione reductase activities of arterial tissue in individuals of various ages *Journal of Geront.* 20: 357-62

KITCHELL, J. *et al.* (1961) Potential uses of chelation methods in treatment of cardiovascular diseases *Prog. Cardiol. Dis.* 3: 238-249

LAMAR, C. (1964) Chelation therapy of occlusive arteriosclerosis in diabetic patients *Angiology* 15: 379-95

LAMAR, C. (1966) Chelation edartectomy for occlusive atherosclerosis *J. Am. Geriat. Soc.* 14: 272-94

LIBERMAN, U. *et al.* (1967) Myositis ossificans traumatica with unusual course effect of EDTA on calcium, phosphorus and manganese excretion *American Journal of Med. Sci.* 254: 35-47

McDONAGH, E., RUDOLPH, C. and CHERASKIN, E. (1981) Serum cholesterol and the ageing process *Medical Hypothesis* 7: 685-94

McDONAGH, E., RUDOLPH, C. and CHERASKIN, E. (1982a) Effect of intravenous EDTA upon blood cholesterol in private practice environment *Journal of Int. Acad. Preventive Medicine* VII (1): 5-12

McDONAGH, E., RUDOLPH, C. and CHERASKIN, E. (1982b) Influence of EDTA salts plus multivitamin-trace mineral therapy upon total serum cholesterol/high density lipoprotein cholesterol *Medical Hypothesis* 9: 643-46

McDONAGH, E., RUDOLPH, C. and CHERASKIN, E. (1982c) Effect of intravenous EDTA plus supportive multivitamin/trace mineral supplementation upon fasting serum calcium *Medical Hypothesis* 11: 431-8

McDONAGH, E., RUDOLPH, C. and CHERASKIN, E. (1982d) Effect of EDTA chelation therapy upon renal function: a study in serum creatinine *Journal of Holistic Medicine* 4 (2): 146-51

McDONAGH, E., RUDOLPH, C. and CHERASKIN, E. (1982e) Homoeostatic effect of EDTA with supportive multivitamin/ trace mineral supplementation upon high density lipoproteins *Journal of Osteopathic Physicians and Surgeons of California* 8 (2): 277-279

McDonagh, E., Rudolph, C. and Cheraskin, E. (1984) Effect of EDTA chelation therapy with multivitamin/trace mineral supplementation upon reported fatigue *Journal of Orthomolecular Psychiatry* 14 (4): 277-9

McDonagh, E., Rudolph, C. and Cheraskin, E. (1985a) The clinical change in patients treated with EDTA chelation multivitamin/trace mineral supplementation *Journal of Orthomolecular Psychiatry* 14 (1): 61-5

McDonagh, E., Rudolph, C. and Cheraskin, E. (1985b) The psychotherapeutic potentials of EDTA chelation *Journal of Orthomolecular Psychiatry* 14 (3): 214-17

Olwin, J. (1968) Reduction of elevated plasma lipid levels in atherosclerosis following EDTA therapy *Proc. Soc. Exper. Biol. Med.* 128 (3-4): 1137-40

Oser, B. *et al.* (1963) Safety evaluation studies of calcium EDTA *Tox. App. Pharm.* 5: 142-62

*Passwater, R. (1981) *Supernutrition for Healthy Hearts* Thorsons

Peng, C. *et al.* (1977) Abnormal mitochondrial oxidative phosphorylation of ischaemic myocardium reversed by calcium chelating agents *Journal of Mol. Cel. Cardiology* 9: 897-908

Perry, H. (1961) Chelation therapy in circulatory and sclerosing disease *Fed. Proc.* 20 (3): Part II Suppl. 10: 254-7

Perry, H. and Schroeder, H. (1955) Depression of cholesterol levels in human plasma following EDTA *Journal of Chron. Dis.* 2 (5) (Nov.): 520-33

Perry, W. (1988) Value of EDTA in atherosclerosis *Royal College of General Practitioners, Members' Reference Book,* pp.213-14

Peters, R. *et al.* (1945) British anti-Lewisite (BAL) *Nature* 156 (3969): 616-19

*Pritikin, N. (1980) *The Pritikin Program for Diet and Exercise* Bantam Books, New York

Rasmussen, H. and Bordier, P. (1974) McDonagh, R., Rudolph, C. and Cheraskin, E. (1982c) Effect of intravenous EDTA plus supportive multivitamin/trace mineral supplementation upon fasting serum calcium *Medical Hypothesis* 11: 431-8

Rubin, M. (1954) 'Metabolic interrelations' Josiah Macy Jr Foundation, Transcript 5th Conference, New York, p.355

Stirling, J. Personal communication to author.

SURAWICZ, B. (1959) Use of chelating agent EDTA in digitalis intoxication and cardiac arrhythmias *Progress in Cardiovascular Diseases* (1959-60) 2: 432-43

SZEKELY, P. *et al.* (1963) Effects of calcium chelation on digitalis induced cardiac arrhythmias *British Heart Journal* 25: 589-94

WALKER, M. and GORDON, G. (1982) *The Chelation Answer* M. Evans & Co., New York

WARTMAN, A. *et al.* (1967) Plaque reversal magnesium EDTA in experimental atherosclerosis *Journal of Atherosclerosis Research* 7: 331

WILDER, L. *et al.* (1962) Mobilization of atherosclerosis plaque calcium with EDTA utilizing the isolation-perfusion principle *Surg.* 52 (5): 793-5

WILLS, E. (1965) Mechanisms of lipid peroxide formation in tissues: role of metals and haematin proteins in catalysis of oxidation of unsaturated fatty acids *Biochem. Biophys. Acta.* 98: 238-51

* Suggestions for further reading

Index